Books for a Small Planet

Typeset in ITC Century and Goudy Old Style Italic by
World Composition Services, Inc., Sterling, Virginia
and printed by
Pantagraph Printing, Bloomington, Illinois USA

Epigraph from *Mop, Moondance, and the Nagasaki Knights*, by Walter Dean Myers.
Copyright 1992 by Dell, a division of Bantam, Doubleday, Dell Publishing Group,
Inc. Reprinted by permission of the publisher.

Helen Kornblum *Director of Communications and Marketing*
Ellen Garshick *Copy Editor*
Ann Kammerer *Cover*

Teachers of English to Speakers of Other Languages, Inc.
1600 Cameron Street, Suite 300
Alexandria, VA 22314 USA
Tel 703-836-0774 ● Fax 703-836-7864

ISBN 0-939791-53-6
Library of Congress Catalog No. 93-061812

Books for a Small Planet

A Multicultural-Intercultural Bibliography for Young English Language Learners

Dorothy S. Brown

Teachers of English to Speakers of Other Languages, Inc.

"Intercultural means that you figure out how somebody's different and let them know that you know it and don't mind too much."

—Mop, in *Mop, Moondance, and the Nagasaki Knights*, by Walter Dean Myers

Contents

Acknowledgments

I wish to express my sincere appreciation to Ron Eckard of Western Kentucky University, Bowling Green, for supplying me with numerous useful book lists and for writing the Foreword. I also thank Dorothy Schnare of Berea College, Berea, Kentucky, for her meticulous proofreading and careful editing. She saved me from making some serious mistakes; I am responsible for any remaining faults.

I am especially obligated to the librarians at the Brentwood Branch of the Springfield, Missouri, Public Library System. With unending patience they helped me locate books (often a time-consuming chore in the Children's Section!), obtained books from the Main Library and other branches, and ordered books for me through interlibrary loan.

I am also indebted to my friend Helen Topham, a volunteer assistant at the Waikiki Branch of the Honolulu Public Library, for her valuable suggestions.

Foreword

For more than 15 years Dorothy S. Brown has been collecting books, writing reviews, and compiling annotations to provide resources for ESL/EFL students. It all started with the germ of an idea she introduced at the 1979 TESOL Convention in Mexico City. With much encouragement from Virginia French Allen, Alice Osman, and others, Dr. Brown eventually developed her compilation into *A World of Books: An Annotated Reading List for ESL/EFL Students* (TESOL, 1988), a book I find myself using time and time again.

Like the earlier volume, *Books for a Small Planet* gives an idea of just how many books have been published recently with a focus on cultural diversity. This book differs from *A World of Books*, however, in that it highlights more recent publications and focuses on children and young adults. It differs greatly also from such works as Eden Ross Nilsen's *Your Reading: A Booklist for Junior High and Middle School Students*, 8th ed. (Urbana, IL: National Council of Teachers of English, 1991) because it cites numerous books that are often overlooked by others. Furthermore, Dr. Brown's crisp, clear annotations and helpful appendixes make this book a unique resource for students, teachers, parents, and librarians.

Books for a Small Planet will be of particular interest to ESL/EFL teachers for a number of reasons. First, it can serve as a guide to selecting appropriate books for students to read outside of class. Extensive reading, whether in one's first or another language, is a good way to learn new vocabulary and develop good reading habits.

Second, the books Dr. Brown has selected are not ESL/EFL books. As trade books, they provide an "authentic" English model for young readers. The books can supplement the workbooks, basic readers, and abridged editions commonly found in ESL/EFL classrooms.

Third, this extensive bibliography can be used to help immigrant students find and select books about people from their native culture. All readers want to see themselves in the characters, settings, and situations that make up their pleasure reading. In *Books for a Small Planet* almost all students should be able to find books with which they can personally identify. And second-generation immigrants can select books that can help them to identify cultural issues, patterns, celebrations, and commemorations that only their parents or grandparents can recall with certainty, thereby providing an important stimulus for communication between generations.

Fourth, as students read and learn more about their native culture, they gather new knowledge to share with fellow students and with teachers. In short, they become experts on culture. I have seen quiet, seemingly shy ESL/EFL students blossom into surprisingly eloquent narrators when given the opportunity to explain their own culture.

Fifth, ESL/EFL teachers can use this bibliography of fiction, nonfiction, and picture books to create a completely communicative class. In keeping with the current emphasis on language learning and teaching for communicative purposes, teachers can devise a number of speaking and writing activities in which the students share their reactions to books without having to rely on the traditional—and often unsuccessful—book report. (See E. Fry, D. Fountoukidis, and J. Polk, eds., "Book Report Alternatives," *The New Reading Teacher's Book of Lists* [Englewood Cliffs, NJ: Prentice-Hall, 1985].)

Resourceful ESL/EFL teachers will discover a variety of other uses for this bibliography. Some may wish to read aloud to their students from the books listed. Others may want to use one book as the beginning of an in-depth research project on a particular culture. Some may ask students to compare two books by the same author or to contrast two accounts by two different authors. Since 18 of the books concern holidays and special occasions, students can compare U.S. holidays with those in other countries. Finally, because most of the books have been recently published, students (perhaps native speakers of English and nonnative speakers of English working together) can write fan letters to their favorite authors. Chances are they will get a response.

Dr. Brown applied the following criteria in deciding which of the many books she read to include in this bibliography:

1. The books should include diverse ethnic settings and characters (including middle-class American).
2. The bibliography should include books appropriate for young people from preschool through high school.
3. Selections should contain little or no dialect, slang, or other expressions that might add to the problems of a student reader.
4. The books should treat ethnic groups and races with respect. (This does not mean, of course, that there must be no evil people in the books!)
5. The books should be in print at the time of the bibliography's publication.

6. The books must be of high literary quality, well written, and interesting. In other words, they must be *good books*.

After compiling bibliographies for more than 15 years and teaching English and ESL/EFL for more than 30 years, Dorothy Brown certainly knows a good book when she reads it.

Ronald D. Eckard
ESL and TESOL Director
Western Kentucky University

A Note From the Compiler

Classifying the books was not easy. Is Roald Dahl's *Minpins* a story (part I) or a fairy tale (part II)? Are *The Hundred Dresses*, by Eleanor Estes, and *Miss Happiness and Miss Flower*, by Rumer Godden, stories (part I) or fiction (part III)? *Anno's Journey* is wordless, but the pictures tell many stories to the attentive observer. Margaret Wise Brown's *Goodnight Moon* contains words and pictures but doesn't tell a story, whereas her other two books do.

For books about language I followed a simple rule, putting those about words in part I and those about morphology (e.g., Marvin Terban's books) or subjects (space, holidays) in part IV.

Except for books published late in 1993, all entries are listed in *Books in Print* for 1992–1993. The publishing business is unpredictable, however, and a book that is in print today may be out of print tomorrow.

Dates given are usually for the most recent edition. When two dates are given, the one in parentheses indicates the book's earliest date of publication, and the second one indicates its most recent edition. Paperback editions are included only when hardcover editions are not available.

Age levels were obtained from *Books in Print*, with some modifications. Ages pertain to reader interest rather than to reading level or linguistic ability.

Children's Books in Print, available in children's bookstores and in some libraries, is an excellent resource for information on publishers of children's books.

Part I

Picture Books, Word Books, and Stories

Andrews, Jan. *The Very Last First Time.* Illustrated with watercolor paintings by Ian Wallace. New York: Macmillan, 1986. 32 pp. K–4.

When the tide is out, the Inuit people of northern Canada walk on the bottom of the sea and gather mussels to eat. Eva Padiyat has often walked there with her mother, but this time, after she and her mother make a hole in the ice, she descends alone to the sea bed. Her fascination with the undersea world, her confidence, her dedication to her job, and her terror when her candle goes out and she hears the tide coming in are all captured in the story and the brilliant illustrations.

Anno, Mitsumasa. *Anno's Journey.* New York: Putnam's (1970), 1981. 48 pp. Grade 4 up.

Like many of Anno's books, this one contains no words, but the pictures contain action and tell stories. Anno arrives in northern Europe in a rowboat and crosses the continent on horseback. He sees people cutting down trees, picking fruit, moving furniture, making and eating cotton candy, rowing a boat, and getting married. Story characters such as Little Red Riding Hood are also pictured, as well as miniature scenes from well-known paintings.

This book can stimulate conversation between two students of differing language backgrounds. It affords countless opportunities for using the English present progressive in pointing out what people *are doing.*

———. *Anno's USA.* New York: Putnam's (1983), 1992. 48 pp. Preschool (PS)–8.

A lone traveler in a small boat approaches the west coast of America. On horseback, he travels across the continent, going backward in time. As he leaves the east coast, the Santa Maria appears over the horizon.

Examples of U.S. art and literature are included. As in all of Anno's books, people are busy. Tom Sawyer is shown watching a friend whitewash the fence for him; students who have read Mark Twain's book translated into their native language may recognize this scene.

Brown, Margaret Wise. *Goodnight Moon.* Illustrated by Garth Williams. New York: HarperCollins (1947), 1991. 34 pp. PS–1.

"Goodnight" is said to the moon, mittens, house, comb, brush, and "nobody," represented by a blank page. Children enjoy naming or finding objects, looking for the tiny mouse on each page, and identifying the pictures on the wall of The Three Bears and of The Cow Jumping over the Moon. The third picture on the wall is an illustration from Brown's *Runaway Bunny.*

————. *The Runaway Bunny.* Illustrated by Garth Williams. New York: HarperCollins (1942), 1991. 32 pp. PS–2.

A baby rabbit threatens to become a fish, a rock, a crocus, a bird, a tree, and more, but his wise mother always dissuades him. Finally he decides to remain her little bunny.

The illustrations are lively, colorful, and humorous.

Also recommended:

————. *Wait Till the Moon Is Full.* Illustrated by Garth Williams. New York: HarperCollins (1948), 1989. 32 pp. PS–3.

Brusca, Maria Cristina. *On the Pampas.* Illustrated by the author. New York: Henry Holt; Markham, Ontario: Fitzhenry & Whiteside, 1991. 30 pp. Grades 2–3.

Related in the first person, this story tells of Maria Christina's summer with her grandparents on their ranch in Argentina. She rides horseback, brushes the horses, swims in the creek, looks for ostrich eggs, and corrals the horses. She also learns to lasso a calf and to dance the *zamba.*

The watercolor illustrations are full of friendly human faces and lively, sometimes apprehensive, animals.

Dorros, Arthur. *Abuela.* Illustrated by Elisa Kleven. New York: Dutton, 1991. 32 pp. PS–2.

Rosalba and her grandmother go by bus to the park and feed the birds. Then Rosalba imagines a trip with her grandmother, flying over Manhattan. They would wave to people waiting outside at a bus stop. They would say "Good morning." They would glide close to the sea, circle the Statue of Liberty, visit the airport, and more. What a pleasant way for young English language learners to practice the English conditional mode!

The brilliant collage illustrations add energy, action, and humor to this exciting trip.

Ernst, Lisa Campbell. *Sam Johnson and the Blue Ribbon Quilt.* Illustrated by the author. New York: Lothrop, 1983. 32 pp. K–3.

While mending a tear in an awning, Sam Johnson discovers his talent for quilting. When he decides to join the Women's Quilting Club, however, he is rebuffed. Quilting, he is told, is women's work. He starts an "Equal Rights for Men" movement, enlists the cooperation of his fellow farmers, and with them creates a prize-winning quilt.

The subtle humor of this timely tale is captured in the illustrations, especially in the alert expressions on the faces of the barnyard animals.

————. *Walter's Tail.* Illustrated by the author. New York: Macmillan, 1992. 40 pp. PS–2.

Mrs. Tully's dog, Walter, can't stop wagging his tail. When he is a puppy, friends and neighbors think he is cute, but as he grows larger his tail becomes more and more destructive. To avoid causing more trouble, Mrs. Tully and Walter climb to the top of a hill, where Mrs. Tully falls. But a clever and devoted Walter signals for help and they are both rescued.

The bold and colorful illustrations reflect a remarkable resemblance between Mrs. Tully and Walter.

Also recommended:

————. *Ginger Jumps.* Illustrated by the author. New York: Macmillan, 1990. 32 pp. PS–2.

————. *Nattie Parsons' Good-Luck Lamb.* Illustrated by the author. New York: Viking, 1988. 32 pp. PS–3.

Flack, Marjorie. *The Story about Ping.* Illustrated by Kurt Wiese. New York: Viking, 1933. Puffin, 1989 (paper). 32 pp. K–2.

Ping, a duck, lives on a boat on the Yangtze River with numerous relatives. He is always careful not to be the last to cross the bridge to the boat, because the last duck gets a spank on the back. One night, to avoid being spanked, he sleeps on the river bank, and the next day finds that his boat has left. After some exciting narrow escapes he finds his boat-home.

The illustrations are simple but lively.

Freeman, Lydia & Don. *Pet of the Met.* Illustrated by the authors. New York: Penguin (1953), 1988. 63 pp. PS–3.

Maestro Petrini, a white mouse, lives in the attic of the Metropolitan Opera House with Madame Petrini and their three children, Doe, Ray, and Mee. While working as a page-turner for the prompter, Maestro Petrini jumps up on the stage and dances during a performance of *The Magic Flute*. Mefisto, the Cat, under the spell of Mozart's music, forgets their enmity and joins the dance.

The illustrations are as whimsical and exciting as the story.

Gibbons, Gail. *Weather Words and What They Mean*. Illustrated by the author. New York: Holiday House, 1990. 32 pp. K–3.

Words such as *temperature, wind,* and *rain* are defined and illustrated. Somewhat technical terms, such as *air pressure* and the names for different types of clouds, are also included. The origin of fog, frost, thunderstorms, and other weather-related phenomena is explained.

Text and pictures are completely integrated, with some of the definitions and weather comments in comic-book-style balloons. The print is large and legible, and the colorful pictures are simple, effective, and clear.

Ginsburg, Mirra. *Asleep, Asleep*. Illustrated by Nancy Tafuri. New York: Greenwillow, 1992. 24 pp. PS up.

With a vocabulary of fewer than 25 words and a great deal of repetition, this book is good for beginning readers or English language learners. Animals, bees, woods, and fields are asleep. Only a child and the wind are awake.

The watercolors are appropriately subdued, and the eyes of the creatures (except the fishes) are closed.

Godden, Rumer. *Fu-Dog*. Illustrated by Valerie Littlewood. London; Ringwood, Victoria, Australia; Markham, Ontario; Auckland; New York: Penguin, 1990. 56 pp. PS–2.

Li-la's Chinese great-uncle sends her a tiny Fu-Dog made of green satin. When her mother, who is half Chinese, tells her that everything Great Uncle touches turns to gold, Li-la decides to go to see him. With her brother Malcolm, she takes Fu-Dog to London, where they find Great Uncle but lose Fu-Dog. The ending, however, is happy.

The illustrations show ugly little Fu-Dog in oriental glory, Li-la with her black hair and oriental eyes, and Malcolm with blonde hair and a skeptical expression.

————. *Miss Happiness and Miss Flower*. Illustrated by Jean Primrose. New York & London: Puffin (1960), 1987. 88 pp. Grades 2–6.

Eight-year-old Nona has been sent from India to live in England with an uncle, his wife, and their children. A package arrives with two Japanese dolls, Miss Happiness and Miss Flower. Belinda, a disagreeable child, does not care for them, but Nona loves them and furnishes the Japanese doll house that her cousin Tom builds for them. The dolls have feelings that they communicate to each other. Their presence brings happiness to Nona and causes some change in Belinda's disposition.

In a sequel, *Little Plum*, a child Nona's age moves next door. She has a Japanese doll who becomes a peacemaker between her arrogant owner and the other children.

Heide, Florence Parry, & Gilliland, Judith Heide. *The Day of Ahmed's Secret*. Illustrated by Ted Lewin. New York: Lothrop, 1990. 32 pp. K–3.

Ahmed is proud that he is strong enough to carry the heavy bottles of butane gas that he delivers to customers in Cairo, proud that he can help his family, and proud of the secret that he will share with them: He has learned to write his name! In Arabic, of course.

The noisy and colorful confusion of the city is skillfully captured in the illustrations.

———. *Sami and the Time of the Troubles*. Illustrated by Ted Lewin. Boston: Houghton Mifflin, 1992. 31 pp. K–4.

Sami lives in Beirut with his grandfather, his mother, and his sister in the basement of his uncle's house. Because of the gunfire on the streets they are often unable to go outside. When they do go out, they clean up the streets, and then Sami and his friend Amir play with improvised wooden guns. Sami has heard stories of a day when hundreds of children marched in the streets carrying signs with the words STOP THE FIGHTING. His family agrees that it is time for another such march.

The vibrant illustrations, many on a background of black, add to the poignancy of this account of a war-torn land.

Hendry, Diana. *A Camel Called April*. Illustrated by Thor Wickstrom. New York: Lothrop, 1991. 48 pp. PS–3.

Six-year-old Harry conjures up animals in his dreams—a lion, a giraffe, monkeys, and April, a camel—and they materialize! He tries to dream the camel back to the Sahara Desert, but April remains in the park, where during the day he gives rides to children. At night April stays in Harry's dreams.

The black-and-white illustrations, like the story, are whimsical.

———. *Christmas on Exeter Street*. Illustrated by John Lawrence. New York: Knopf, 1989. 32 pp. K–3.

Just before Christmas an old house fills up with relatives and friends bringing gifts, pets, babies, food, and party hats. They sleep in beds, in the bathtub, on window sills, on shelves, in the kitchen sink, even on the mantel.

The spirit of generosity is captured in this story of an amazing house where there is always room for one more.

The ink and watercolor illustrations emphasize the good nature of hosts and guests.

Also recommended:

————. *The Not Anywhere House.* Illustrated by Thor Wickstrom. New York: Lothrop, 1991. 47 pp. PS–3.

Hewett, Joan. *Laura Loves Horses.* Illustrated with photographs by Richard Hewett. New York: Clarion, 1990. 40 pp. Grades 2–5.

Eight-year-old Laura Santana's home is a California horse farm where her father works. On Saturday she rides Sugar Baby and helps groom another horse. Later, at a horse show, she rides Perriwinkle, a Thoroughbred, in the class for children 12 and under. Perriwinkle and his little rider take the jumps smoothly and come in third.

The beautiful full-page illustrations in this photo-essay show Laura riding Sugar Baby, then Perriwinkle, then Sugar Baby again, this time dodging waves at the ocean's edge.

Knight, Margy Burns. *Talking Walls.* Illustrated by Anne Sibley O'Brien. Gardiner, ME: Tilbury, 1992. 32 pp. K–8.

Pictured and described here are memorial walls, cave walls, decorated cliffs, prison walls, a prayer wall, and more from all over the world: Egypt, China, Zimbabwe, Peru, Mexico, Canada, Israel, South Africa, France, Australia, the United States. One, in Berlin, has been torn down. Some are beautifully decorated by artists, some with graffiti and pictures by amateurs. One, the Great Wall of China, can be seen from the moon.

The text and the large, vibrant pastel illustrations are closely integrated.

Leaf, Munro. *The Story of Ferdinand.* Illustrated by Robert Lawson. New York: Viking, 1936. 61 pp. PS–2.

When men come to select the roughest bull to fight in the bull fight, peace-loving Ferdinand, stung by a bee, jumps, snorts, and paws the ground. Thinking him the fiercest of all, the men take him to Madrid, where he sits down quietly in the bull ring and sniffs at the flowers the ladies wear in their hair.

For over half a century children (and adults) have read or listened to this minitreatise on peace.

The black-and-white illustrations are lively and comical.

MacDonald, Suse. *Alphabatics.* Illustrated by the author. New York: Macmillan, 1986. 56 pp. PS–1.

In this unique ABC book each letter changes its position until it becomes a completed picture on the opposite page. The J, for example, turns into a jack-in-the-box; K turns into a kite. Some of the letters actually evolve into the object: The M becomes a mustache and the S becomes a swan. Though the acrobatic concept remains clever and creative throughout the book, some letters may be difficult to "see" in their final evolution; for instance, the *kite* is a backward K, and the rain around *umbrella* is an inverted U.

Maestro, Betsy. *Delivery Van: Words for Town and Country.* Illustrated by Giulio Maestro. New York: Houghton Mifflin, 1990. 32 pp. PS–2.

The careful driver of the van is Pat, a young woman. She delivers packages to a *hardware store*, a *pharmacy*, the *town hall*, the *library*, the *school*, and other places. She picks up a package at the antique shop, and on her route she passes a *bank*, a *movie theater*, and other places. This book is useful for increasing word recognition.

The colorful, uncluttered illustrations afford many opportunities for discussion.

———. *Taxi: A Book of City Words.* Illustrated by Giulio Maestro. New York: Houghton Mifflin, 1989. 29 pp. PS–3.

Each page contains a large picture with one or two sentences beneath it containing a single-word or two-word concept (*taxi, office building*). A busy yellow taxi takes passengers to a *railroad station*, a *zoo*, a *pier*. It drives over a *bridge* and through a *tunnel*.

This is an excellent word concept book, with simple text and clear, colorful pictures.

Also recommended, for learning prepositions and adverbs:

———. *Where Is My Friend? A Word Concept Book.* Illustrated by Giulio Maestro. New York: Crown, 1986. 32 pp. PS–1.

Mansell, Dom. *If Dinosaurs Came to Town.* Illustrated by the author. Boston, Toronto, London: Little, Brown, 1991. 26 pp. PS–3.

Numerous kinds of dinosaurs are shown. They obstruct traffic in town, startle livestock in the country, splash through water, and fly near planes. The brief text on each double page describes these prehistoric reptiles and defines their long and difficult names. *Triceratops*, for example, means "Three-horn-face."

Young dinosaur buffs will appreciate the humor in the elaborately cluttered double-page cartoons.

Most, Bernard. *The Littlest Dinosaurs.* Illustrated by the author. San Diego, New York, London: Harcourt Brace Jovanovich, 1989. 30 pp. PS–3.

Not all dinosaurs are huge. In this picture book those that are 13 feet long are humorously described and pictured as the size of a seesaw, a slide, or a garage. A 12-foot dinosaur is as long as a diving board. At 10 feet, one is slightly longer than a bus-stop shelter. Others are compared to and pictured with a sofa, a station wagon, and other objects. The smallest, 8 inches, is smaller than a teddy bear.

The illustrations, like the text, are simple and clear. All are in color.

————. *There's an Ant in Anthony.* Illustrated by the author. New York: William Morrow (1980), 1982. 32 pp. PS up.

After Anthony finds an *ant* in his name, he finds it in pl*ant*, hydr*ant*, eleph*ant*, and in other words. His search takes him to many interesting places, including the zoo and the North Pole.

The black ink line drawings are appropriately simple, and the ants can't be missed. They are red.

Parish, Peggy. *Amelia Bedelia.* Illustrated by Fritz Siebel. New York: Harper, 1963. 32 pp. K–4.

Amelia Bedelia takes language literally. When told to change the towels in the bathroom, she cuts them. Directed to dust the living room, she sprinkles dust on everything in it. To draw the drapes, she takes a pencil and paper and draws a picture of them. Her ridiculous responses are good lessons in the ambiguity of the English language.

The cartoonlike illustrations show Amelia constantly busy and always smiling.

Children (and adults) who like this kind of wackiness can also find it in *Thank You, Amelia Bedelia*; *Teach Us, Amelia Bedelia*; and other sequels.

Polacco, Patricia. *Appelemando's Dreams.* Illustrated by the author. New York: Putnam's, 1991. 32 pp. PS–3.

Appelemando shares his large and colorful dreams with four good friends, but his dreams upset the townspeople. When the children lose their way in the forest, they signal for help with a brightly colored dream and are rescued by the villagers, who then become proud of the bright dreams that cover the paths and walls of their town.

The illustrations show the village and villagers in somber shades and the dreams in contrasting bright colors.

————. *Mrs. Katz and Tush.* Illustrated by the author. New York: Bantam, 1992. 30 pp. Grades 2–4.

Larnel, an African-American boy, gives a kitten to Mrs. Katz, a lonely Jewish widow from Poland. They become friends, celebrate Passover together, and Mrs. Katz tells Larnel of similarities in their ancestral background: the slavery of Jews in Israel and of Africans in America and the segregation of and discrimination against both groups. When Tush, the kitten, grows up, they rejoice in the birth of her kittens.

The warm relationship of the woman, the boy, and the cat is shown in the illustrations as well as in the story.

Sakade, Florence, ed. *Japanese Children's Favorite Stories.* Illustrated by Yoshisuke Kurosaki. Rutland, VT; Tokyo: Charles E. Tuttle, 1953 (1st ed.), 1958 (rev. ed.), 1992 (41st printing). 120 pp. Grades 1–4.

In this collection of stories anything can happen. A kettle walks a tightrope, sparrows and monkeys dance, goblins reach out long distances with their noses, a sparrow becomes a woman, the man in the moon changes into a beggar, toothpicks turn into swords for tiny warriors, and a spider weaves fleecy white clouds. In some stories goodness is rewarded; in others, evil characters reform.

The illustrations, many of them in color, are delicate, lively, and amusing.

Say, Allen. *The Bicycle Man.* Illustrated by the author. Boston: Houghton Mifflin, 1982. 48 pp. K–3.

At a small village in occupied Japan, children have just completed their Sportsday activities when two U.S. soldiers appear. One has red hair; the other has "a face as black as the earth." The African American borrows the principal's bicycle and performs amazing tricks with it, to the delight of the teachers as well as children. This simple story is a touching example of interracial harmony.

The soft pastel colors, the expressive faces, and the constant activity of children and adults in the illustrations add warmth and excitement to the story.

Scarry, Richard. *Richard Scarry's Best Busy Year Ever.* Racine, WI: Western, 1991. 70 pp. PS–3.

Animals dressed as children play games. Their elders garden, water flowers, clean streets, and much more. A pig family goes on a fourth of

July picnic. Children enjoy a circus. Thanksgiving, Christmas, and a birthday are celebrated. The activities seem endless.

All of Scarry's books can be used with profit by language learners of any age.

————. *Richard Scarry's Best Word Book Ever.* Racine, WI: Western (1963), 1988. 70 pp. PS–3.

Scarry's word/picture books are excellent vocabulary builders. This one shows Bear washing his face, brushing his teeth, combing his hair, and more. We are shown what he eats for breakfast, apparently not just for one day but for at least a week! Subsequent pages show the interior of the Rabbit family's house, toys, tools, and an airport. Everything is clearly labeled.

Also recommended:

————. *Richard Scarry's Busiest People Ever.* New York: Random House, 1976. 45 pp. PS–2.

Sendak, Maurice. *Pierre: A Cautionary Tale.* Illustrated by the author. New York: Harper, 1962. 48 pp. PS–3.

Pierre responds to his parents' greetings, reprimands, offers of food, invitations, and threats with one sentence, "I don't care." Only after being swallowed by a lion and surviving does he say, "I care."

The black-and-white illustrations, like the repetitious story, will make children laugh. Some children, after hearing this book read aloud, have been known to emulate Pierre's speech behavior for hours, or even days, afterwards, thus perhaps amusing their language teachers but annoying their parents.

Tompert, Ann. *Grandfather Tang's Story: A Tale Told with Tangrams.* Illustrated by Robert Andrew Parker. New York: Crown, 1990. 32 pp. PS–2.

A tangram is a puzzle made of a square cut into seven standard pieces with which pictures can be formed. Grandfather Tang and Little Soo have seven pieces each, which Grandfather Tang arranges to illustrate a story about two foxes who change themselves into a dog, a squirrel, a hawk, a turtle, a crocodile, a goldfish, a goose, a lion, and finally back to foxes. Their adventures as they pursue each other and play tricks are exciting.

The watercolor illustrations match, in form, the small black tangram shapes.

————. *The Silver Whistle.* Illustrated by Beth Peck. New York & London: Macmillan, 1988. 32 pp. K–3.

With money for the clay whistle he has made and sold, Miguel plans to buy a silver whistle to place on the manger on the day before Christmas. Instead, he generously sacrifices his money, but the Holy One is pleased with the simpler gift of a yellow clay bird.

The illustrations depict the soft colors of the U.S. southwest, the multi-colored clothing and serapes of the Mexicans, and the reverence of the people.

Van Laan, Nancy. *A Mouse in My House.* Illustrated by Marjorie Priceman. New York: Knopf, 1990. 32 pp. PS–3.

The house is inhabited not only by a mouse, but also by a cat, a dog, a snake, a bug, a fish, an ape, a bear, a pig, and a lion, each visible only to the young narrator. Rhythm, rhyme, and repetition make this an entertaining read-aloud book.

The lively watercolor illustrations add to its charm.

Wallace, Ian. *Chin Chiang and the Dragon's Dance.* Illustrated by the author. New York: Macmillan, 1984. 32 pp. K–4.

Chin Chiang has long dreamed of dancing the dragon's dance on the first day of the Year of the Dragon. But when the day comes he is afraid that he cannot dance well enough to make his grandfather proud of him. With the help and encouragement of a newfound friend, he overcomes his fear and gains skills and confidence.

The bright watercolor illustrations are packed with action.

Weiss, Nicki. *On a Hot, Hot Day.* Illustrated by Monica J. Weiss. New York: Putnam's, 1992. 32 pp. PS–2.

Mama and Angel are shown keeping cool in the hot summer, drinking cocoa in the rainy fall, walking in the snow in winter, and breathing the fresh air in spring. Rhyme, images, and gentle humor make this an excellent read-aloud book. Mama and Angel are Hispanic, and so is the community in which they live: The sign on the grocery store says *El Bodegero.* But signs with *cheese, tuna,* and *ice cubes* indicate that they live in the United States.

The illustrations are simple enough to appeal to very young children.

Yashima, Taro. *Umbrella.* Illustrated by the author. New York: Viking, 1958. 33 pp. PS–1.

Momo is given red rubber boots and an umbrella for her third birthday. She impatiently waits for a rainy day, when she pulls on her boots, takes her umbrella, and goes outside.

The colorful pictures show Momo at home and outside in the rain, protected by her umbrella.

Yee, Paul. *Tales from Gold Mountain: Stories of the Chinese in the New World.* Illustrated with paintings by Simon Ng. Originally published by Groundwood Books, Toronto. New York: Macmillan, 1989. 64 pp. Grades 2–5.

These eight stories are set in Canada and the United States over 100 years ago, when men came from China to work on railroads, as farmers, and at other jobs. Their lives were hard, and they suffered. Each of these stories, however, has a happy ending. Many contain supernatural events, but all are about the virtue, industry, and resourcefulness of Chinese immigrants.

Though written in the tradition of folktales, the stories were all invented by the same author.

Yolen, Jane. *All Those Secrets of the World.* Illustrated by Leslie Baker. Boston, Toronto, London: Little, Brown, 1991. PS–3.

Four-year-old Janie's cousin Michael, who is five, explains to her that the ships on the horizon look small because they are far away. When Janie's father returns from war and observes how much she has grown, she wisely explains to him that she is bigger because he has been far away and now he is closer.

The theme is reflected in the watercolor illustrations, which range from close-ups of the family to panoramic scenes of land and sea.

Part II

Legends, Fables, Folktales, and Fairy Tales

Aardema, Verna. *Anansi Finds a Fool.* Illustrated by Bryna Waldman. New York: Dial, 1992. 32 pp. PS–3.

Anansi looks for a partner to go fishing with him, one who will do all the work while Anansi takes all the fish. His friend Bonsu agrees to that. arrangement, but outwits Anansi. Their sensible wives laugh together heartily at their husbands' behavior.

The double-page illustrations, in delicate colors, are notable for the expressive faces of the characters.

————. *Traveling to Tondo: A Tale of the Nkundo of Zaire.* Illustrated by Will Hillebrand. New York: Knopf, 1991. 30 pp. K–4.

When a civet cat starts walking to Tondo to be married, he is joined by a pigeon, then a python, then a tortoise. They delay him so much that when he reaches Tondo his bride-to-be has married someone else. The story has humor, rhythmic repetition, and a timely lesson.

In addition to large pictures of the civet cat and his three friends, small silhouettes of the four animals walking to Tondo decorate many pages of the text.

Also recommended:

————. *Oh Kojo! How Could You!* Illustrated by Marc Brown. New York: Dial, 1984. 32 pp. PS–3.

————. *Pedro and the Padre: A Tale from Jalisco, Mexico.* Illustrated by Friso Henstra. New York: Dial, 1991. 32 pp. PS–3.

————. *Who's in Rabbit's House?* Illustrated by Leo & Diane Dillon. New York: Dial, 1977. 32 pp. PS–3.

Allen, Linda. *The Giant Who Had No Heart.* Illustrated by the author. New York: Putnam's, 1988. 40 pp. PS–3.

When his six older brothers leave home to look for brides, Ashiepattle stays at home with their father the king. The six do not return, so Ashiepattle sets out to look for them. With the aid of a raven, a salmon, and a wolf he rescues his brothers and their brides and finds a bride for himself.

The delicate watercolors are lively and whimsical. Even the salmon has an expressive face.

————. *The Mouse Bride: A Tale from Finland.* Illustrated by the author. New York: Putnam's, 1992. 32 pp. PS–3.

A father plants a tree for each of his three sons. When the trees and the boys are grown, he cuts down a tree for each son; each young man then seeks his bride by following the direction in which his tree has fallen. The youngest son finds a clever little mouse that, in the best tradition of such stories, turns into a beautiful princess.

The typically Scandinavian, soft pastel watercolors capture the spirit of the story. The self-assured expression on the face of the mouse is appropriately regal.

Belpré, Pura. *Perez and Martina: A Porto Rican Folk Tale.* Illustrated by Carlos Sanchez. New York & London: Frederick Warne (1930), 1963. 56 pp. PS–3.

Martina, a pretty Spanish cockroach, has many suitors: Señor Cat, Señor Cock, Señor Duck, Señor Cricket, Señor Frog, and Señor Perez the Mouse. When each proposes marriage to her, she asks him to tell her how he will talk to her in the future. She declines the proposal of each one except Perez. After they are married, Perez meets a truly tragicomic fate. Martina still weeps for him.

The large, brightly colored illustrations show these creatures gaudily but tidily dressed, with wonderful, expressive faces.

Breckler, Rosemary K. *Hoang Breaks the Lucky Teapot.* Illustrated by Adrian Frankel. Boston: Houghton Mifflin, 1992. 32 pp. K–3.

Hoang has inherited his mother's teapot, the family's most precious treasure. When his family moves into their new home in America, after leaving Vietnam, young Hoang breaks it. He is afraid that bad luck will chase him and his family back into the sea, but he patiently and creatively solves the problem.

The illustrations, in subtle shades of brown and yellow, have a dream-like quality.

Bryan, Ashley. *The Cat's Purr.* Illustrated by the author. New York: Macmillan, 1985. 42 pp. PS–3.

According to this story from the West Indies, Cat and Rat were once friends. But Cat's uncle gives him a tiny drum that makes a soothing sound if stroked gently. He tells Cat to let no one else play it. Cat discovers Rat playing the drum, though he has been told not to touch it. They fight, and during their scuffle Cat accidentally swallows the drum. If you rub a cat gently, you hear the purr of the little drum. But Cat and Rat, of course, are no longer friends.

The brown ink illustrations show the emotions of Cat, his uncle, and Rat not only in their faces but also in their body language.

————. *Turtle Knows Your Name.* Illustrated by the author. New York: Macmillan, 1989. 32 pp. PS–2.

Upsilimana Tumpalerado has a long name, but his Granny's name is even longer. Granny tells him he cannot have dessert until he learns her name. This story from the West Indies is filled with rhythmic repetition, fun, and humor.

The brilliant watercolor illustrations also have humor, as well as action and a rhythm of their own.

Climo, Shirley. *The Egyptian Cinderella.* Illustrated by Ruth Heller. New York: HarperCollins, 1989. 32 pp. K–3.

The setting for this variation of a universally well-known story is Egypt in the 6th century BC. The heroine is Rhodopis, a blonde Greek girl who has been sold as a slave to the Egyptians. Her slippers are made of leather gilded with rose-red gold. One of them is stolen by a falcon and dropped into the lap of the Pharaoh, who then finds Rhodopis and makes her his queen.

The illustrations are rich, striking, and brilliant, if sometimes gaudy.

————. *The Korean Cinderella.* Illustrated by Ruth Heller. New York: HarperCollins, 1993. 39 pp. K–3.

Pear Blossom is mistreated by her stepmother and her stepsister. At the village festival she accidentally drops one of her sandals into the water. It is retrieved by a magistrate, who finds Pear Blossom and proposes marriage. Of course they live happily ever after.

The detailed double-page illustrations are dramatic and brilliant.

Also recommended:

————. *King of the Birds.* Illustrated by Ruth Heller. New York: HarperCollins, 1988. 32 pp. K–3.

This legend is ancient and widespread. It is known in many European countries and also among the Chippewa Indians of North America.

Compton, Patricia A. *The Terrible Eek: A Japanese Tale.* Illustrated by Sheila Hamanaka. New York, London, Toronto, Sydney, Singapore: Simon & Schuster, 1991. 40 pp. K–3.

While the wind blows and the rain batters at the house, a father tells his son that what he fears most is "a terrible leak." A thief on the roof thinks the father said "a terrible eek," and a wolf thinks that "a terrible leak" means a thief. While they flee in terror, the boy and his parents sleep peacefully in their dry beds. The excitement and humor in this action-packed book, shown in the illustrations as well as in the text, are the result of misunderstandings.

Dahl, Roald. *Minpins.* Illustrated by Patrick Benson. New York: Viking, 1991. 47 pp. Grades 2–4.

Little Billy visits the Forest of Sin, where tiny people called Minpins live inside trees, wear suction boots that enable them to walk up and down branches, and travel on the backs of birds. Riding on the back of a swan, Billy saves them from the horrible Red-Hot Smoke-Belching Gruncher. Children who like fantasy and excitement will find plenty of both in this story.

The illustrations are strikingly brilliant and exciting, while at the same time delicate.

Day, David. *The Sleeper.* Illustrated by Mark Entwisle. Nashville, TN: Ideals Children's Books, 1990. 32 pp. K–4.

Wu Wing Wong, the youngest monk in the monastery, cannot get enough sleep. After the Emperor decrees that all libraries be emptied, Wu is sent to deliver the monastery's books to the palace. On the way he takes refuge in a cave and does not wake up for 200 years. The Emperor has burned all the other books and the country is in turmoil. But Wu has with him the Book of Ancestors, which proves which king should be emperor, and order is restored. After his 200-year nap, Wu no longer needs so much sleep.

The watercolor illustrations show Wu sleeping, moving books, and riding a horse. When he is in the cave, the pictures have an unreal, dreamlike quality.

De Gerez, Toni. *Louhi, Witch of North Farm.* Illustrated by Barbara Cooney. New York: Viking, 1986. 32 pp. PS–3.

In this Finnish legend Louhi, witch of the Far North, steals the sun and the moon, plunging the land into total darkness. When she sees Seppo, a smith, forging iron chains and an iron collar to restrain her, she becomes frightened and replaces these heavenly bodies.

The full-page and double-page illustrations capture the awesome beauty of the North.

Demi. *The Empty Pot.* Illustrated by the author. New York: Henry Holt; Markham, Ontario: Fitzhenry & Whiteside, 1990. 32 pp. PS–2.

An emperor who loves flowers gives seeds to all the children in the land and proclaims that the child who can show him the best plant will succeed him to the throne. Ping, who plants his seed carefully, transplants it many times, and tends it faithfully, has only an empty pot to show the emperor. But he is rewarded for his honesty.

The delicate, brightly colored watercolors of the children and the emperor are as enchanting as the story.

————. *The Magic Boat.* Illustrated by the author. New York: Henry Holt; Markham, Ontario: Fitzhenry & Whiteside, 1990. 32 pp. PS–2.

The boy Chang is given a magic boat by an old man he has rescued from the river. Chang uses the boat to rescue an ant, a bee, a crane, and a wicked man named Ying. Ying steals the boat, but Chang retrieves it with the help of his three friends.

The illustrations, with the generous use of red and gold characteristic of Demi's work, appear in a bubblelike circle on each page.

Also recommended:

————. *Chen Ping and His Magic Axe.* Illustrated by the author. New York: Dodd, Mead, 1987. 32 pp. K–3.

————. *Liang and the Magic Paintbrush.* Illustrated by the author. New York: Henry Holt, 1987. 32 pp. K–3.

De Paola, Tomie. *The Legend of the Indian Paintbrush.* Illustrated by the author. New York: Putnam's, 1988. 40 pp. PS–2.

This Native American tale tells how a wild flower that grows in the western United States, especially in Texas and Wyoming, got its name. The author's note at the end will interest adults and older children.

The illustrations are strikingly beautiful.

———. *Tony's Bread: An Italian Folktale.* Illustrated by the author. New York: Putnam's, 1989. 32 pp. PS–3.

Occasional Italian words, translated immediately into English, add spice to this fable of a baker whose daughter marries a nobleman after he persuades her father to set him up in business in Milan.

The illustrations are suitably amusing.

Also recommended:

———. *The Legend of the Bluebonnet: An Old Tale of Texas.* New York: Putnam's, 1983. 32 pp. PS–3.

Esbensen, Barbara Juster. *Ladder to the Sky: How the Gift of Healing Came to the Ojibway Nation.* Illustrated by Helen K. Davis. Boston, Toronto, London: Little, Brown, 1989. 29 pp. PS–3.

Long ago, people were healthy and no one died. This legend begins when spirit messengers carried old people to the sky by means of a magic vine. When the spirit messengers take a young man, his grandmother climbs the vine, falls to earth, and brings disease and death to the people. But the Ojibway people then learn to cure sickness and disease with plants.

French, Fiona. *Anancy and Mr. Dry-Bone.* Illustrated by the author. Boston, Toronto, London: Little, Brown, 1991. 24 pp. PS–3.

In this story based on characters from African and Jamaican folktales, poor Anancy and rich Mr. Dry-Bone both want to marry Miss Louise. She declares that she will marry the man who makes her laugh. Anancy wins, simply by looking ridiculous in the clothes he has borrowed from his animal friends.

The illustrations are stylized and brilliant.

Ginsburg, Mirra. *The Chinese Mirror.* Illustrated by Margot Zemach. San Diego: HarBrace, 1988. 26 pp. PS–3.

This Korean story tells of a man who goes to China, buys a mirror, and takes it home with him. Each member of his family looks into it without recognizing his or her own face. The result is an entertaining little domestic comedy.

The large watercolor illustrations are typically Korean.

Goble, Paul. *Crow Chief: A Plains Indian Story.* Illustrated by the author. New York: Orchard, 1992. 28 pp. PS–2.

Long ago, when crows were white, people hunted buffalo with spears and arrows. Crow Chief would warn the buffalo when hunters were coming, and the hunters were unable to get near them. When the hungry people prayed for help, a young man called Falling Star helped them to outwit Crow Chief, whose feathers became black with soot from the cooking fires.

The colorful illustrations are strikingly brilliant.

————. *The Great Race of the Birds and Animals.* Illustrated by the author. New York, Toronto, Oxford, Singapore, Sydney: Macmillan, 1991. 26 pp. K–3.

In this Cheyenne and Sioux myth, people and birds race against animals to decide whether people will eat buffalo or buffalo will eat people. The race is won by a clever Magpie, and the chiefs of the Buffalo Nation graciously admit defeat. The Creator then advises the people to use their power wisely.

The double-page illustrations are as exciting as the story.

Greene, Jacqueline Dembar. *What His Father Did.* Illustrated by John O'Brien. Boston: Houghton Mifflin, 1992. 32 pp. K–3.

With one kopek, Herschel sets out from the village of Minsk to visit his elderly aunt in the village of Pinsk. By a clever ruse he not only reaches Pinsk but eats and sleeps well on his way. Herschel's escapade and his final revelation of what his father did will amuse readers young and old.

The colorful illustrations add to the rollicking humor of the story.

Haugaard, Erik Christian. *Prince Boghole.* Illustrated by Julie Downing. New York: Macmillan, 1987. 32 pp. K–3.

Three princes come to Munster, on the island of Eire (Ireland), to woo the king's daughter. Each is told to return a year later and bring back a bird, and the prince with the fairest fowl can marry the princess. The ending is predictable, but the occasional wry humor makes up for the triteness of the plot.

The double-page illustrations depict people, beasts, and birds in a colorful medieval setting.

Hong, Lily Toy. *How the Ox Star Fell from Heaven.* Illustrated by the author. Morton Grove, IL: Whitman, 1991. Toronto: General Publishing, 1991. 32 pp. K–3.

In this humorous tale, oxen live in heaven. Because there is no beast of burden on earth to help them grow food, the peasants have little to eat. When the Emperor of Heaven sends the Ox Star to earth with a message for the peasants, he distorts it. Because of his stupid mistake, he is hurled from heaven and becomes a beast of burden.

Kherdian, David. *Feathers and Tails: Animal Fables From Around the World.* Illustrated by Nonny Hogrogian. New York: Philomel, 1992. 95 pp. Grade 1 up.

Nineteen fables and two proverbs, each from a different source or country, make up this collection. Like humans, the birds and animals are kind, cruel, smart, stupid, clever, gullible, brave, cowardly, lazy, or industrious. And no matter in what part of the world the stories originate, the humanlike behavior is the same.

The illustrations, most in soft shades, some in deeper colors, depict animals with humanlike expressions: inquisitive, apprehensive, serious, surprised, haughty, quizzical, self-satisfied, concerned, amused.

Kirstein, Lincoln. *Puss in Boots.* Illustrated by Alain Vaës. Boston, Toronto, London: Little, Brown, 1992. 32 pp. PS–3.

This familiar story of the cleverest cat in literature is told with appropriate flourish and illustrated with operatic glamor. Children unfamiliar with the story will find it exciting, and all readers, or listeners, will be captured by the full-page dramatic illustrations in brilliant colors.

The author is one of the founders of the New York City Ballet, and the illustrator is a painter who has designed sets for that ballet company and others.

Lagerlof, Selma. *The Changeling.* Translated from the Swedish by Susanna Stevens. Illustrated by Jeanette Winter. New York: Knopf, 1992; Toronto: Random House of Canada, 1992. 28 pp. K–5.

A troll woman exchanges her ugly child for a human baby. The human mother, though grieving for her own child, takes good care of the ugly and disagreeable troll. Her kindness is rewarded in the end, when her son is returned to her and she learns that her treatment of the troll has saved her own son's life.

The terror, worry, and love of the human mother and the understandable impatience of her husband are shown in the beautiful, colored illustrations.

Laird, Elizabeth. *The Road to Bethlehem: An Ethiopian Nativity.* Illustrated with pictures from manuscripts in the British Library. New York: Promo Books, 1987. (paper) 32 pp. Grades 1–5.

This version of the Christmas story is set in Ethiopia. It tells of the three wise men, of King Herod, of the Holy Family's flight into Egypt, and more, some of which will be unfamiliar to readers of the account in the Bible.

The illustrations show characters, furniture, animals, and people as typically Ethiopian. Subtle shades of green, brown, tan, blue, and orange predominate.

Loverseed, Amanda. *Tikkatoo's Journey: An Eskimo Folktale.* New York: Peter Bedrick, 1990; London: Blackie & Sons, 1990. 32 pp. PS–4.

Nanook, the village's oldest and wisest man, is ill. Only fire from the sun can save him. Tikkatoo, his grandson, bravely travels beneath the seas and up to the sun, returning with a flame that saves his grandfather.

The illustrations show the cold of the north, the loneliness of the moon, the heat of the sun, and the constant movement under the sea.

Mayer, Marianne. *The Little Jewel Box.* Illustrated by Margo Tomes. New York: Puffin, 1990. 30 pp. PS–3.

When Isabel is about to go out into the world to seek adventure, her mother accidentally bakes her a bad-luck cake instead of a good-luck cake. Her father gives her a jewel box and tells her to open it only when in danger of death. After many narrow escapes and frequent use of the little box, Isabel marries her true love.

Unlike most fairy tales, this one is witty. In fact, it can be read as a parody of traditional stories. The artist has captured the author's humor in the illustrations.

————. *The Sorcerer's Apprentice: A Greek Fable.* Illustrated by David Wiesner. New York, Toronto, London, Sydney, Auckland: Bantam, 1989. 64 pp. Grade 3 up.

Alex, a young orphan, becomes an apprentice to Bleise, a sorcerer who can make objects do his bidding. Alex tends the herb garden, while household chores are done by the sorcerer's magic. Alex studies his master's books and learns how to make a broom and bucket fetch water. But the broom gets out of control, more brooms with buckets materialize, and the result is a disastrous mess; however, all turns out well in the end.

The watercolor illustrations capture the magic and the comedy of the story.

Also recommended:

————. *The Prince and the Princess: A Bohemian Fairy Tale.* Illustrated by Jacqueline Rogers. New York, Toronto, London, Sydney, Auckland: Bantam, 1989. 64 pp. Grade 3 up.

Newton, Pam. *The Stonecutter: An Indian Folktale.* Illustrated by the author. New York: Putnam's, 1990. 32 pp. PS–3.

A stonecutter wants to be, and becomes, first a rich man, then a king, then the sun that burns the king, a cloud that shades the sun, wind that blows the cloud, and a mountain that cannot be moved by wind, sun, king, or wealth. At the end he becomes a contented stonecutter again, making building blocks from the stones taken from the mountain.

The exotic illustrations, inspired by paintings from India, create a suitable setting for this story.

Oughton, Jerrie. *How the Stars Fell into the Sky: A Navajo Legend.* Illustrated by Lisa Desimini. Boston: Houghton Mifflin, 1992. 32 pp. K–3.

While First Woman is writing the laws in the sky so that all the people can read them, Coyote offers to help. But he impatiently flings the remaining stars into the night in disarray. Not knowing the laws, the people remain confused.

The dramatic illustrations, in rich, deep shades of blue, amber, and green, show the beauty of desert and sky, the impatience of Coyote, and the final despair of First Woman.

Paterson, Katherine. *The King's Equal.* Illustrated by Vladimir Vagin. New York: HarperCollins, 1992. 64 pp. Grades 2–5.

Prince Raphael's father, the king, tells the prince that he cannot become king until he marries a woman who is his equal in beauty, intelligence, and wealth. After the king dies, the self-centered prince sends his councilors to find him a wife. Their search and the prince's reaction to each princess are related with humor and suspense. The prince is finally united with a woman of the required qualifications, but not until he has learned some valuable lessons.

The text, by a world-renowned U.S. author, and the brilliant illustrations, by a distinguished Russian artist, combine to make this an exquisite story with a modern feminist theme.

Schwartz, Howard, & Rush, Barbara. *The Diamond Tree: Jewish Tales from Around the World.* Illustrated by Uri Shulevitz. New York: HarperCollins, 1991. 120 pp. Grades 2–5.

In these 15 tales and legends, nine geographical areas are represented: Palestine, Iraq, Turkey, Yemen, Morocco, Poland, Babylon, the Orient, and eastern Europe. Some include characters from the Old Testament. Some resemble familiar fairy tales. Most celebrate universal virtues such as honesty, wisdom, cooperation, charity. Some, which reflect the gullibility and foolishness of humans, are wildly comic.

The comic elements are emphasized in the spectacular illustrations.

Shannon, George. *Stories to Solve: Folktales From Around the World.* Illustrated by Peter Sis. New York: Greenwillow, 1985. 56 pp. Grades 3–5.

These 14 folktales are from the United States, Africa, Tibet, Armenia, Ethiopia, Japan, China, and some unnamed sources. Each brief story ends with a problem to be solved by the reader. The correct answer can be found by turning the page.

Stories and solutions are illustrated with lively drawings.

Also recommended:

————. *More Stories to Solve: Fifteen Folktales From Around the World.* Illustrated by Peter Sis. New York: Greenwillow, 1990. 64 pp. Grades 3–5.

Steptoe, John. *Mufaro's Beautiful Daughters: An African Tale.* Illustrated by the author. New York: Lothrop, 1987. 32 pp. K–3.

Mufaro's two daughters are both beautiful. Nyasha is also kind, but Manyara is selfish and bad-tempered. When the king announces that he wants a wife, Mufaro prepares to go before him with both his daughters. Manyara, hoping to gain advantage by arriving first, slips ahead of her father and sister. On her way to the king she refuses to give food to a hungry child and is rude to others whom she meets. Nyasha, because of her kindness and generosity, is chosen by the king.

The elaborately detailed illustrations, in glowing colors, were inspired by the ruins of an ancient city in Zimbabwe.

Tejima, Keizaburo. *Ho-Limlim: A Rabbit Tale from Japan.* Illustrated by the author. New York: Putnam's, 1990. 34 pp. PS–3.

This folktale is from the Ainu people, who live on the northernmost island of Japan, Hokkaido. It is about an aging rabbit whose eyes play tricks on him as he travels from place to place. He learns that when one gets old, it is better to stay home than to venture out.

The bold, multicolored woodcut illustrations add vigor and drama to the story.

Van Laan, Nancy. *Rainbow Crow: A Lenape Tale.* Illustrated by Beatriz Vidal. New York: Knopf, 1989. 40 pp. PS–2.

When the snow and cold arrive, a brave crow flies up to the Great Sky Spirit and brings the gift of fire back to the animals. The crow's reward is freedom from being hunted, captured, or eaten.

The double-page watercolor illustrations exhibit an unusual combination of delicacy and strength.

Wang, Rosalind C. *The Fourth Question: A Chinese Tale.* Illustrated by Ju-Hong Chen. New York: Holiday House, 1991. 32 pp. PS–3.

Yen-Lee is told by a Wise Man that he may ask one or three questions, but not two or four. Instead of asking his own questions, he generously asks questions for three other people. In the best tradition of folktales, his unselfishness is rewarded.

The illustrations, intricate in design and delicate in color, have an oriental flavor.

Watkins, Yoko Kawashima. *Tales From the Bamboo Grove.* Illustrated by Jean and Mou-sien Tseng. New York, Toronto, Oxford, Singapore, Sydney: Macmillan, 1992. 49 pp. Grades 4–11.

These six folktales were among those told to the author when she was a child living in North Korea. Some were told by her parents, others by guests in their home. Each story has a theme or moral, usually subtle.

The mood of each story is captured in a black-on-white watercolor illustration.

Winthrop, Elizabeth. *Vasilissa the Beautiful: A Russian Folktale.* Illustrated by Alexander Koshkin. New York: HarperCollins, 1991. 38 pp. Grades 1–5.

With the help of a doll given to her by her mother, a beautiful young girl survives the cruelty of her stepmother, her stepsisters, the witch Baba Yaga, and more. As always in fairy tales, the ending is happy.

The full-page and double-page illustrations are luminous, dramatic, and colorful.

Yacowitz, Caryn. *The Jade Stone: A Chinese Folktale.* Illustrated by Ju-Hong Chen. New York: Holiday House, 1992. 32 pp. PS–3.

Chan Lo, who always carves what a stone tells him it wants to be, carves three playful carp from a piece of jade, even though the Emperor has commanded him to carve a dragon. The Emperor at first is angry, but he rewards the carver for his courage and integrity.

The illustrations are ink and watercolor paintings prepared on hand-made rice paper. They are uniquely beautiful as well as suitably comic.

Yen, Clara. *Why Rat Comes First: The Story of the Chinese Zodiac.* Illustrated by Hideo C. Yoshida. San Francisco: Children's Book Press, 1991. 32 pp. K–5.

The Jade King of Heaven invites thousands of animals to a feast, but only 12 arrive. He decides to name each year after one of the guests: rat, ox, tiger, hare, dragon, snake, horse, sheep, monkey, rooster, dog, and boar. This cheerful little fable resolves the argument between rat and ox, who both claim to be deserving of first place in the zodiac.

The colorful illustrations are bold and humorous.

Yolen, Jane. *The Seeing Stick.* Illustrated by Remy Charlip & Demetra Maraslis. New York: Crowell; Toronto: Fitzhenry & Whiteside, 1977. 32 pp. K up.

The Emperor's daughter, Hwei Ming, is sad because she cannot see. Her father offers a fortune in jewels to anyone who can restore her sight. Monks, magician-priests, and physicians try without success. Then an old man with a walking stick on which he whittles portraits teaches her to see with her fingers.

The drawings in wax and pencil are first in black and white, then in damasklike tones to signify the restoration of Hwei Ming's sight.

Young, Ed. *Lon Po Po: A Red Riding Hood Story from China.* Illustrated by the author. New York: Putnam's, 1989. 32 pp. K–4.

When their mother leaves to visit their grandmother, three children are left alone in the house. Then the wolf arrives, disguised as the grandmother, Po Po. The children recognize the wolf, however, and cleverly trick him.

The illustrations, in watercolors and pastels, have a mystical, dreamlike quality.

Part III

Fiction

Baillie, Allen. *Little Brother.* Scotland: Blackie & Sons, 1985; Ringwood, Victoria, Australia: Penguin, 1990; New York: Viking Penguin, 1992. 144 pp. Grades 3–7.

Eleven-year-old Vithy becomes separated from his 18-year-old brother Mang as they flee the Khmer Rouge in Cambodia. With courage and resourcefulness, Vithy makes his way alone to the Thai border, where he serves as interpreter and helper to an Australian woman doctor and continues to search for his brother.

British-Australian spelling (e.g., *tyre*) and some unfamiliar vocabulary (e.g., *cyclo*) may puzzle readers in the United States but probably won't interfere with comprehension.

Baker, Carin Greenberg. *Fight for Honor* (Karate Club 1). New York; Ringwood, Victoria, Australia; Toronto; London; Auckland: Penguin, 1992. 136 pp. (paper) Grades 3–7.

Lee, born in Vietnam and adopted by a U.S. couple with two other sons, is the young hero of this story about the tenets of karate: Use it for defense only and try to settle problems without fighting. Lee's brothers and his antagonistic classmates force him to make some difficult choices.

A glossary of Japanese words used in karate is included.

Other books in this series are *High Pressure*, *Road Warriors*, *Girl Trouble*, and *Out of Control*.

Banks, Lynne Reid. *The Indian in the Cupboard.* New York: Doubleday, 1985. 181 pp. Grades 4–7.

Omir, a boy living in London, puts a toy Indian in an old bathroom cupboard, which he then locks with a magic key. The next day he opens the cupboard and finds that the toy has turned into a tiny, live 18th-century American Indian named Little Bear, with bow and arrow. The problem is how to keep this Indian, and others who materialize later, a secret and protect them from exploitation by adults.

This exciting adventure story has two sequels: *The Secret of the Indian* and *The Return of the Indian*.

Berleth, Richard. *Samuel's Choice.* Illustrated by James Watling. Niles, IL: Whitman, 1990. 38 pp. Grades 3–6.

Samuel, a 14-year-old slave, is the narrator. He helps General Washington's troops cross the water from Long Island to Manhattan and escape the British soldiers who are pursuing them. Samuel's owner, who is sympathetic to the British, turns all of his property, including Samuel and other slaves, over to the U.S. troops so that he will not be taken prisoner. Thus Samuel becomes free.

The Battle of Long Island was the first battle in the American Revolution.

Blume, Judy. *Tales of a Fourth Grade Nothing.* Illustrated by Roy Doty. New York: Dutton, 1972. 120 pp. Grades 2–3.

This humorous story is narrated by Peter Hatcher, a fourth-grader, whose little brother Fudge (real name Farley Drexel) is more than his parents can handle. Long-suffering Peter must constantly come to their rescue. He is resourceful. He is also, understandably, a bit self-righteous.

Two sequels, also narrated by Peter, are *Superfudge* and *Fudge-a-Mania.*

Buck, Pearl S. *The Big Wave.* Illustrated with prints by Hiroshige and Hokusai. New York: HarperCollins (1947), 1986. 78 pp. A 1993 paperback edition does not include the illustrations. Grades 3–6.

To Kino, a Japanese boy whose father is a farmer, the sea is beautiful. To his friend Jiya, whose father is a fisherman, it is an enemy. When a big tidal wave approaches, Jiya is sent out of danger by his parents and takes refuge with Kino's family. His parents and brother perish in the wave, and Jiya becomes a part of his friend's family. This is a poignant story of danger and courage.

The prints by two famous Japanese artists are appropriate but unfortunately not in color.

Carter, Dorothy Sharp. *His Majesty, Queen Hatshepsut.* Illustrated by Michele Chessare. New York: Lippincott, 1987. 248 pp. Grade 5 up.

The narrator is Hatshepsut, princess, then queen-regent, then pharaoh, at a time when queen rulers were seldom tolerated. As a girl, she is sulky, restless, arrogant, and impatient but at times remorseful. She becomes, however, a resolute and powerful ruler.

This fictionalized account of a real Egyptian queen is a fascinating introduction to life in ancient Egypt. It may, however, present some difficulties to a reader. The use of archaic terms such as *thou, thee,* and *mayst,* and the many characters and places with strange names, make this book slow but rewarding reading.

The glossary of characters and gods is helpful.

Choi, Sook Nyul. *Year of Impossible Goodbyes.* Boston: Houghton Mifflin, 1991. 169 pp. Grade 5 up.

Sookan tells of her childhood in occupied Korea. Almost 10 years old, she must attend Japanese school, where she is forbidden to speak Korean and is physically mistreated, as are the other Korean children. Even worse is the lack of food for her family. When World War II ends, the Japanese leave and the Russians arrive. At first conditions improve, but soon Russian propaganda, forced labor, and the lack of freedom become as oppressive as the conditions during the Japanese occupation.

The escape of Sookan and her little brother Inchun, especially after they become separated from their mother, is the exciting climax of this historical novel.

Cleary, Beverly. *The Mouse and the Motorcycle.* Illustrated by Louis Darling. New York: William Morrow, 1965. 108 pp. Grades 2–6.

Keith and his parents stop in California at the Mountain View Inn, where Keith makes friends with Ralph, a young mouse who enjoys riding Keith's toy motorcycle. Ralph and his large extended mouse family will charm readers young and old.

The black-and-white illustrations capture the story's excitement and humor.

. Ralph continues to ride his motorcycle and to have adventures in two sequels: *Runaway Ralph* and *Ralph S. Mouse.*

————. *Muggie Maggie.* Illustrated by Kay Life. New York: William Morrow, 1990. 70 pp. Grades 3–5.

Maggie Schultz is a stubborn and arrogant third grader who refuses to learn to read and write cursive. Her teacher considers her "not motivated," while Maggie considers herself "gifted and talented." Maggie's classmates watch with fascination while she steadfastly revolts. They are amused when she tries to write her name in cursive and it turns out to be *Muggie*. With the aid of other teachers, Maggie's teacher cleverly tricks her into learning to write cursive.

Conrad, Pam. *Pedro's Journal: A Voyage with Christopher Columbus.* Illustrated by Peter Koeppen. Honesdale, PA: Caroline House, 1991. 80 pp. Grades 3–7.

This historical novel is written in the form of a diary by a sensitive cabin boy, Pedro de Salcedo, who travels with Columbus on his first voyage to the New World. He tells of the fears and discontent of the seamen, the excitement of sighting land, and the capture of the gentle native inhabitants. There is irony in the account of the treatment of the natives and more than a touch of distaste for Columbus's arrogance.

The skillfully executed black-and-white illustrations, supposedly drawn by Pedro, are appropriate for this perceptive novel.

Cormier, Robert. *Tunes for Bears to Dance To.* New York: Delacorte, 1992. 101 pp. Grade 5 up.

Henry has many problems. His older brother, Eddie, has died; his father needs therapy for depression; his mother is overworked; and Henry works after school for a grocer who is mean, dishonest, intolerant, and cruel. Henry makes friends with Jacob Levine, a mentally disturbed Jewish wood-carver who is a victim of the Holocaust in Germany, and with George Graham, who directs the rehabilitation center where Mr. Levine goes every day to work on his carving. Henry is tempted to solve his family's problems at a terrible price.

Crew, Linda. *Children of the River.* New York: Delacorte, 1989. Dell (paper), 1991. 213 pp. Grade 7 up.

Thirteen-year-old Sundara flees Cambodia with relatives. They settle in a small Oregon town, where Sundara has to adjust to U.S. ways without offending her aunt, who is afraid that her niece will become too American-ized. Sundara also struggles with an inner conflict, as she wrongly blames herself for the death of her aunt's baby.

Dahl, Roald. *Esio Trot.* New York & London: Viking, 1990. 64 pp. Grades 3–7.

This amusing story contains some elements of a fairy tale: the love of Mr. Hoppy for Mrs. Silver, her devotion to her little tortoise, Alfie, and the unusual way in which Mr. Hoppy, with the help of 140 other tortoises, wins her admiration. The book contains and condones trickery, but there is none of the violence typical of Dahl's early books.

————. *Matilda.* New York & London: Viking, 1988. 224 pp. Grades 3–7.

At the age of four, Matilda has read books by Faulkner, Hemingway, Dickens, and Hardy, but her mother and father are unaware of her brilliance. Through her cleverness and her supernatural powers, she overcomes all obstacles, both hers and those of her beloved teacher, Miss Honey. Here is a combination of sentiment and absurdity that will amuse some young readers but may confuse others.

Dorris, Michael. *Morning Girl.* New York: Hyperion, 1992. 74 pp. Grades 3–5.

Twelve-year-old Morning Girl, who loves the day, and her younger brother Star Boy, who loves the night, take turns narrating this novel about a Taino family living on an island in the Caribbean in 1492. The father, mother, and two children are depicted as intelligent, witty, and thoughtful.

The epilogue, a letter in which Christopher Columbus describes these people as "very poor in everything," is a powerful jolt of irony to the reader.

Estes, Eleanor. *The Hundred Dresses.* Illustrated by Louis Slobodkin. New York, Toronto, London, Auckland, Sydney: Harcourt Brace, 1944. 78 pp. Grades 1–5.

Wanda Petronski, who wears the same dress to school day after day, tells her classmates that she has 100 dresses hanging in her closet. They do not believe her, and they tease her about the 100 dresses and also about her strange Polish name. But when a drawing contest is held, Wanda wins the prize. Her classmates recognize her talent and regret their behavior.

Garrigue, Sheila. *The Eternal Spring of Mr. Ito.* New York: Bradbury, 1985. Toronto: Collier Macmillan, 1985. 163 pp. Grades 5–7.

Because of the bombing of England during World War II, Sara has been evacuated and is living with her relatives in Canada. Mr. Ito, a native of Japan but loyal to Canada, works as a gardener for Sara's uncle. When Japan bombs Pearl Harbor, the Ito family is sent, along with others of Japanese ancestry, to an internment camp. Sara's loyalty to the Ito family, especially to Mr. Ito, is the theme of this sensitive novel.

Sara's English friends speak a Cockney dialect. Although their speech may confuse readers, a complete understanding of what they say is not essential for a reader's enjoyment of the book.

George, Jean Craighead. *My Side of the Mountain.* New York: Dutton (1959), 1988. 166 pp. Grades 3–7.

Young Sam Gribley leaves his home in New York City to live alone in the Catskill Mountains, without modern tools or equipment. For shelter, he carves out the rotting part of the trunk of a tree. He makes clothes of deer hide lined with rabbit fur. His food is fish, venison, rabbit, frogs' legs, turtle soup, dandelion, and other delicacies. He trains a falcon, which he names Frightful, to hunt with him.

This young, modern-day Robinson Crusoe is always calm and resourceful, but his account is exciting.

————. *On the Far Side of the Mountain.* New York: Dutton, 1990. 170 pp. Grades 3–7.

In this sequel to *My Side of the Mountain,* Sam is joined by his 13-year-old sister, Alice, who is every bit as resourceful as Sam is. She is also mischievous. She runs away from Sam, leaving clues so that he can find her. Equally important as Sam's search for Alice is the fate of Frightful, whom Sam reluctantly frees at the end, knowing that the bird is an endangered species.

Godden, Rumer. *The Valiant Chatti-maker.* Illustrated by Jeroo Roy. New York: Viking, 1983 (paper). 64 pp. Grades 3–7.

After drinking too much toddy, the Chatti-maker accidentally captures the Tiger and becomes a hero. His consequent good fortune is attained with the help of his Clever Little Wife. He is most happy, however, making his chattis (pots), which have become works of art.

This humorous story is set in India and based on an old Indian folktale. The illustrations, many in color, are both funny and magnificent.

Griffin, Peni R. *Otto from Otherwhere.* New York: Macmillan, 1990. 182 pp. Grades 4–7.

Otto, a musical alien from outer space, is befriended by Paula and her brother Peter, both earthlings living in San Antonio. They help him pass as a visitor from Brazil, where Portuguese is spoken. Otto, of course, does not speak Portuguese, but neither do any of Paula's and Peter's classmates. Many of them speak Spanish, however, so that language would have been a dangerous choice. Otto must make cultural adjustments, as his planet is vastly different from ours.

Hamilton, Virginia. *The House of Dies Drear.* New York: Macmillan (1968), 1984. 246 pp. Grades 6–9.

Thirteen-year-old Thomas Small and his family move from North Carolina to Ohio, where they live in an enormous house once owned by an abolitionist, Dies (rhymes with *flies*) Drear. Once a station on the Underground Railroad, the house contains secret rooms and escape tunnels.

All the characters are African American, some with Native American blood.

————. *The Mystery of Drear House: The Conclusion of the Dies Drear Chronicle.* New York: Greenwillow, 1987. 217 pp. Grade 7 up.

Uncounted treasure is found in the Dies Drear house, and Thomas's father, a college history professor, must decide what to do with it. This sequel to *The House of Dies Drear* is filled with mystery, terror, and animosity, but in the end harmony and peace prevail.

Haugaard, Erik Christian. *The Boy and the Samurai.* Boston: Houghton Mifflin, 1991. 221 pp. Grades 5–9.

Set in feudal Japan, this historical novel is about a street urchin whose mother dies at his birth and whose father is killed in battle. The people who care for him call him *Saru,* meaning "monkey." After he is separated from them, he becomes skillful at surviving on his own. He has many adventures and eventually helps plan and execute the rescue of the samurai's wife.

This is an exciting story about a few gentle and kind people living at a time of greed, cruelty, and senseless fighting.

————. *The Samurai's Tale.* Boston: Houghton Mifflin, 1984. 234 pp. Grade 7 up.

Taro, the brave but sensitive hero and narrator, is the son of a poor samurai who has died in battle. He becomes a servant in the household of an important nobleman, then a samurai and a trusted aide. Set in 16th-century Japan, this fast-paced novel is about duty, loyalty, and peace as well as courage.

Hesse, Karen. *Letters from Rifka.* Richmond Hill, Ontario: Fitzhenry & Whiteside. New York: Henry Holt, 1992. 148 pp. Grades 4–7.

In September 1919, Rifka and her family flee Russia because they are Jews and subject to persecution. They go first through Poland, then to Belgium, where Rifka must be left behind because of illness. Unable to emigrate with her family, she is cared for by kind strangers until she is able to leave; then she is detained on Ellis Island when she reaches the United States. As she travels, she writes to a cousin she has left behind.

Rifka's letters tell a moving story and reflect the courage and fortitude of the young writer. They are based on the experiences of the author's aunt.

Ho, Minfong. *The Clay Marble.* New York: Farrar, Straus, 1991. 163 pp. Grade 7 up.

The narrator is 12-year-old Dara. With her mother and her brother she flees from their village in war-torn Cambodia to a refugee camp at the Thai border. There she meets Jantu, a girl a little older than she is, who fashions dolls and other toys out of clay. The clay marble that Jantu gives Dara seems to have mystical power. When soldiers appear, the two girls and their families must flee again.

The irony of war is not missed in this sensitive novel: Children are killed or lost and people go hungry while soldiers eat the much-needed rice and "fight for peace."

———. *Rice without Rain*. New York: Lothrop, 1990. 236 pp. Grade 7 up.

The setting is Thailand in the 1970s. Four university students spend their vacation in the village of Maekung with the purpose of helping the villagers. But when the villagers are persuaded to protest the payment of half their rice crop to their landlord, the result is tragic.

This novel is rich in symbolism and irony. The central image is rice, the crop on which the villagers depend.

Hoban, Russell. *The Mouse and His Child*. Illustrated by Lillian Hoban. New York: Harper, 1967. 182 pp. Grades 1–5.

Some of the animal characters are real; some are toys. A toy mouse and his son, fastened together, dance when they are wound up. Their greatest wish is to be self-winding. Because of their helplessness, many misfortunes befall them.

This philosophical and thought-provoking fable is filled with suspense and drama.

Irwin, Hadley. *Kim/Kimi*. New York: Macmillan, 1987. 200 pp. Grade 7 up.

Sixteen-year-old Kim Andrews is also Kimi Yogushi. Her natural father was Japanese American, and she has been adopted by her stepfather. To learn about her natural father, she goes to Sacramento and visits nearby Tule Lake, site of a relocation center for Japanese Americans during World War II. Accustomed to feeling conspicuous in the small Iowa town where she lives, Kim experiences culture shock in multicultural California.

Kim is an avid reader of insipid teenage novels about blonde, blue-eyed girls. In the early chapters her reading tastes are amusingly parodied. This is a perceptive book, with gentle touches of irony.

Johnston, Norma. *The Delphic Choice*. New York: Macmillan, 1989. 203 pp. Grade 7 up.

The title refers to the Greek oracle at Delphi. Most of the action, however, takes place in Turkey, where more than once a character must choose, without the help of an oracle, between public good and private safety, between the welfare of all and the safety of one. Meredith, an American girl visiting Quaker relatives, becomes involved in the search for her kidnapped uncle. She also finds romance in this multicultural environment.

Krumbold, Joseph. . . . *and now Miguel.* Illustrated by Jean Charlot. New York: Crowell, 1954. 245 pp. Grade 5 up.

Miguel's older brother Gabriel can get what he wants, and for his younger brother, Pedro, whatever he has is enough. Or so believes Miguel, who is 12 and envies them both. Miguel wants to go into the Sangre de Cristo Mountains, where his father, his older brothers, and other workers take the family's sheep in the summer to graze. How Miguel gets his wish, and the price he has to pay for it, is the subject of this engrossing account of a hard-working Mexican-American family.

Lord, Betty Bao. *In the Year of the Boar and Jackie Robinson.* Illustrated by Marc Simont. New York: Harper & Row; Toronto: Fitzhenry & Whiteside, 1984. 169 pp. Grades 3–7.

Sixth Cousin, known to her Chinese family as Bandit, adopts the name Shirley Temple before leaving China with her mother to join her father in the United States. There, Shirley Temple Wong makes friends, takes piano lessons, and develops a passion for baseball. Although she adapts well to her new environment, she retains her affection for her native land.

This autobiographical novel is written with humor that readers of all cultural backgrounds can appreciate.

Lowry, Lois. *Number the Stars.* Boston: Houghton Mifflin, 1989. 137 pp. Grades 4–7.

Told from the point of view of Annemarie Johansen, whose best friend is Ellen Rosen, a Jewish girl, this historical novel celebrates the courage and ingenuity of the people in Denmark who helped Danish Jews escape to Sweden during World War II. At great risk to herself, 10-year-old Annemarie helps Ellen and her family leave by boat. The solidarity of young Danes in the Resistance movement, and the devotion of all Danes to their brave and defiant King Christian, are inspiring.

Menotti, Gian Carlo. *Amahl and the Night Visitors.* Illustrated by Michelle Lemieux. New York: William Morrow, 1986. 64 pp. PS up.

Adapted by Menotti from his opera, which was first produced in 1951, this story of the visit of the three wise men to a little crippled boy and the miracle that ensued has universal appeal. The rich, warm watercolors show the wise men according to tradition: one African, one Oriental, one Caucasian. Their faces are startlingly expressive, as are those of the boy and his mother.

Morpurgo, Michael. *Waiting for Anya.* New York; London; Toronto; Ring-
    wood, Victoria, Australia; Auckland: Penguin, 1990. 172 pp. Grades 4–6.

Jo's father has gone to fight in World War II. Jo remains with the rest
of his family in a French mountain village near the Spanish border. A few
kilometers away, the Widow Horcada and her Jewish son-in-law, Benjamin,
hide Jewish children who have escaped from occupied Poland and France,
and Benjamin waits hopefully for the return of Anya, his daughter, who
has been separated from him. Jo and Benjamin devise an elaborate but
dangerous plan to help the children escape into neutral Spain.

This novel's fast pace and numerous characters may confuse some
readers, but it is never boring.

Myers, Walter Dean. *Me, Mop, and the Moondance Kid.* Illustrated by
    Rodney Pate. New York: Delacorte, 1988. 150 pp. Grades 3–7.

Eleven-year-old T. J. (for Tommy Jackson) is the narrator. After seeing
the movie *Butch Cassidy and the Sundance Kid,* T. J.'s younger brother
calls himself the *Moondance Kid.* Mop (Miss Olivia Parish) is one of the
best baseball players on the Elks team. Moondance is good, too. T. J. can't
hit, catch, or throw, but he is skillful at rationalizing his shortcomings.

Readers familiar with baseball will find this book exciting. It contains
nonstandard English, which probably won't interfere with comprehension,
but perhaps young ESL students should be advised not to emulate T. J.'s
language, at least not on inappropriate occasions.

————. *Mop, Moondance, and the Nagasaki Knights.* New York: Delacorte,
    1992. 150 pp. Grades 3–7.

Members of the Elks, a Little League baseball team, hope to win a trip
to Japan by first winning a special tournament with visiting teams from
Mexico, France, and Japan. Communication is difficult and often confusing.
T. J. thinks that Stefan, from France, has challenged him to a duel. Mop,
in talking with the Japanese players, agrees to take on a sumo wrestler.
But there are no hard feelings. In fact, the Elks get along well with the
foreigners. It's the members and the coach of another U.S. team who give
the Elks a hard time.

Naidoo, Beverly. *Journey to Jo'burg: A South African Story.* Illustrated
    by Eric Velasquez. New York: Lippincott, 1985. 80 pp. Grades 4–7.

Thirteen-year-old Naledi and her 9-year-old brother leave their grandmother's house and start to walk to Johannesburg, 300 kilometers away,
to tell their mother that their little sister is ill. With the help of a kind truck
driver, they reach their destination. They have some narrow escapes, and

after she learns how Blacks are treated, Naledi begins to think about her own future and what can be done to help her people.

In the sequel, *Chain of Fire*, 15-year-old Naledi and her classmates encounter brutal violence when they try to march peacefully to protest the threatened removal of their families from their homes.

Namioka, Lensey. *The Coming of the Bear.* New York: HarperCollins, 1992. 230 pp. Grade 7 up.

Zenta and Matsuzo, two *ronin* ("unemployed samurai"), are stranded on an island inhabited by Ainu, members of a race despised and feared by the Japanese. Relations between the Ainu and a Japanese settlement on their island are dangerously tenuous. The attempts of Zenta and Matsuzo to prevent war and to promote tolerance and understanding between the two different cultures make this a novel with depth as well as excitement.

———. *Yang the Youngest and His Terrible Ear.* Illustrated by Kees de Kiefte. Boston, Toronto, London: Little, Brown, 1992. 134 pp. Grades 3–7.

When Yingtao's family moves to Seattle from China, he has two problems: playing second violin in the family quartet and mastering the English language. With the help of his musically talented friend Matthew, he solves the problem of his lack of musical talent and discovers that he does have a talent for baseball. His solution is ridiculous and unbelievable, but very funny.

Neugeboren, Jay. *Poli: A Mexican Boy in Early Texas.* Illustrated by Tom Leamon. San Antonio: Corona, 1989. 123 pp. Grade 7 up.

This is a story of a lasting friendship between two young boys: Poli, a Mexican, and Eagle Blood, a Comanche. The Comanches have to protect themselves from Mexicans, from Americans, and from other Indian tribes being pushed south and west by the U.S. government. Even though they have become blood brothers, Poli and Eagle Blood know that they may have to fight against each other.

The poignant ending is inevitably tragic.

O'Dell, Scott. *Island of the Blue Dolphins.* Boston: Houghton Mifflin (1960), 1990. 184 pp. Grade 5 up.

Based on an actual occurrence, this novel tells of Karana, an Indian girl stranded on an island off the coast of California when she was 12 years old and rescued 10 years later. Her self-reliance, her courage, her ingenuity, and her companionship with the wild creatures make this novel exciting.

A sequel, *Zia*, tells of her rescue and her problems with adjusting to living among people.

————. *My Name Is Not Angelica*. Boston: Houghton Mifflin, 1989. 130 pp. Grades 5–9.

Sixteen-year-old Raisha is tricked by a neighboring African tribe, sold to a slave trader, and shipped to an island in the Danish West Indies, where she is cruelly treated and runs away from her owner. This chilling story of fear, courage, resourcefulness, and persistence is based on a slave revolt in 1733.

Paterson, Katherine. *The Master Puppeteer*. Illustrated by Haru Wells. New York: Crowell (1975), 1991. 179 pp. Grade 7 up.

Jiro, an apprentice puppeteer, is the protagonist of this novel set in Japan during a period of famine and lawlessness. While his mother is starving and his father has joined a band of lawless men, Jiro uncovers the identity of Saburo, a mysterious bandit who helps the hungry people of Osaka.

Always exciting, sometimes sad, this story is spiced with humor.

————. *Rebels of the Heavenly Kingdom*. New York: Dutton, 1983. 229 pp. Grade 7 up.

Set in 19th-century China during the Taiping Rebellion, this historical novel tells of a peasant boy, Wang Lee, who is kidnapped and then rescued by a crusading army, which includes a large contingent of woman warriors.

The reader is not spared the horrors and brutality of war as seen through the eyes of Wang Lee, who grows in sensitivity as well as in courage.

Also recommended:

————. *The Sign of the Chrysanthemum*. New York: Crowell (1973), 1991. 132 pp. Grade 7 up.

Sacks, Margaret. *Beyond Safe Boundaries*. New York: Dutton, 1989. 156 pp. Grade 7 up.

Eleven-year-old Elizabeth, who was very young when her mother died, welcomes the stepmother that her father brings to their home in South Africa. But her older sister, Evie, resents their stepmother. There is family friction, but the theme of the novel is much larger than family relationships. It is the complex political and social climate of South Africa and the relations there among Europeans, Africans, Colored (part white, part African), East Indians, and others.

Say, Allen. *The Inn-Keeper's Apprentice.* New York: Harper & Row, 1979. 185 pp. Grade 7 up.

Kiyoi, the son of a Korean father and a Japanese mother, develops his artistic talent and matures socially and emotionally under the guidance of a famous cartoonist in Tokyo. Set in postwar Japan, this unusual novel is based on the early life of the author.

Schlein, Miriam. *The Year of the Panda.* Illustrated by Kam Mak. New York: Crowell, 1990. 96 pp. Grades 3–7.

A boy in China adopts an orphaned baby panda and cares for it. When he learns why pandas are an endangered species and what the government is doing to save them, he dutifully but reluctantly releases his pet to government authorities. The ending is satisfying to the boy, the government, and the panda.

The novel is based on an actual occurrence.

Stolz, Mary. *King Emmett the Second.* Illustrated by Garth Williams. New York: Greenwillow, 1991. 56 pp. Grade 2 up.

Emmett Murphy has problems. His parents are moving from New York City to Ohio, and he has to go along with them. His pet pig, King Emmett, has died. Much to his embarrassment, his mother buys him a bike with training wheels. He has no friends in Ohio. But when Cruz Ramirez, who lives across the street, befriends him, he stops hating his new home. And then something even better happens: He acquires another pet.

The wry humor and gentle understanding of Emmett's parents make this a refreshingly different story of U.S. family life.

Uchida, Yoshiko. *A Jar of Dreams.* New York: Macmillan, 1981. 144 pp. Grades 5–7.

Eleven-year-old Rinko Tsujimura feels out of place in Oakland, California, because she is Japanese. She wants to be like everyone else. Also, her parents must struggle hard during the Depression of the 1930s. But Aunt Waka arrives from Japan and helps the family members face their problems.

There are two sequels: *The Best Bad Thing* and *The Happiest Ending.*

Watkins, Yoko Kawashima. *So Far from the Bamboo Grove.* New York: Lothrop, 1986. 183 pp. Grade 6 up.

In 1945 the author was 11 years old, living in northern Korea. Her father was an official of the Japanese government, working in Manchuria and coming home to his family when he could. Because of the war, Yoko, her mother, and her sister Ko fled from their home in Korea and encountered, on their way to Japan, all the horrors of war. They suffered from hunger and exhaustion and cold, and witnessed rape and death. Yoko and her brave, resourceful older sister reached their native country, but their mother died on the way.

This is a fictionalized account of the author's actual experience.

Whelan, Gloria. *Goodbye, Vietnam.* New York: Knopf, 1992. 136 pp. Grades 3–7.

Mai, the 13-year-old narrator, flees Vietnam with her family on an overcrowded boat. Mai's father rescues from the sea a boy who is the only survivor of a pirate attack on another refugee-laden boat. Then the boy is largely responsible for getting their boat to Hong Kong. A Vietnamese woman doctor helps the sick in a cholera epidemic on board and barely escapes being sent back to Vietnam.

This is a sad but exciting fictionalized account, with a happy ending for the main characters.

Yep, Laurence. *The Star Fisher.* New York: William Morrow, 1991. 150 pp. Grade 3 up.

The title refers to a story that a Chinese-American girl, Joan Lee, tells to her sister Emily, about a golden kingfisher that is transformed into a beautiful woman who reluctantly agrees to marry a farmer. Like the kingfisher, members of the Lee family feel out of place when they move from Ohio to West Virginia. But with the help of the friendly woman who owns the property where they live, they adjust to their new home.

Part IV

Nonfiction

Ashabranner, Brent. *Always to Remember: The Story of the Vietnam Veterans Memorial.* Illustrated with photographs by Jennifer Ashabranner. New York: Dodd, Mead, 1988. 100 pp. Grade 6 up.

The idea for a memorial to honor all U.S. veterans who died or are missing in Vietnam was conceived by Jan C. Scruggs, a veteran haunted by the memory of friends who were killed. The wall was designed by Maya Lin, a Yale student whose parents were refugees from China.

The emotional impact of the wall is captured in the text and in the black-and-white photographs.

Batherman, Muriel. *Before Columbus.* Illustrated by the author. Boston: Houghton Mifflin (1981), 1990 (paper). 32 pp. K–3.

The first people to arrive in what is now called North America were hunters who walked across a strip of dry land that connected northern Asia with that continent. Their hunting weapons, the caves in which they lived, and their buried skeletons have been found. Later there were the Basketmakers, who made pottery, built houses of clay villages called *pueblos*, and planted crops. They took from the land only what they needed to live.

Behrens, June. *Gung Hay Fat Choy: Happy New Year.* Illustrated with photographs compiled by Terry Behrens. Chicago: Childrens Press, 1982. 31 pp. Grades 1–4.

The Chinese New Year festival, which may last as long as 7 days, is celebrated between mid-January and mid-February. The exact dates vary from year to year. Each year is named after one of the 12 animal symbols in the Chinese zodiac. The event is celebrated with fire crackers, parades, carnivals, and gifts. It is observed by Chinese families living in many large cities in the United States as well as in China.

Blumberg, Rhoda. *Commodore Perry in the Land of the Shogun.* Illustrated with reproductions from museums, libraries, art institutes, and other sources. New York: Lothrop, 1985. 128 pp. Grade 4 up.

In 1853, Commodore Perry's ship terrified the Japanese when Perry entered the harbor hoping to open trade with Japan. In spite of frequent misunderstandings, the United States and Japan developed an amicable relationship, accompanied in part by a bit of duplicity on each side: Commodore Perry called himself Admiral; a Japanese police chief assumed the role of governor; governors of provinces were presented as princes.

————. *The Remarkable Voyages of Captain Cook.* Illustrated with reproductions from various sources. New York: Bradbury. Toronto, Oxford, Singapore, Sydney: Maxwell Macmillan, 1991. 137 pp. Grade 4 up.

In the 18th century Captain James Cook made three voyages to the South Seas, exploring the Pacific Ocean. Cook discovered Australia, New Zealand, Tahiti, Hawaii, and more. Because of his careful attention to their diet, most of his men survived the lengthy trips.

Although Cook usually maintained good relations with people everywhere, on his third voyage he became less tactful and was killed in Hawaii.

Branley, Franklyn M. *Neptune: Voyager's Final Target.* New York: HarperCollins, 1992. Illustrated with photos. 56 pp. Grades 3–6.

In 1989, the space probe *Voyager 2* began its encounter with Neptune, a cold (330° below zero) dark planet, fourth largest in our solar system. It had taken *Voyager 2* 12 years to travel the more than 4 billion miles. Much has been learned from the trip: for example, Neptune has 1,000-mile-an-hour winds and many storms. The largest storm, called the Great Dark Spot, is as big as the earth.

The description of this enormous planet and its satellites is enhanced by photographs, most in color.

Brown, Tricia. *Lee Ann: The Story of a Vietnamese American Girl.* Black-and-white photographs by Ted Thai. New York & Canada: Putnam's, 1991. 48 pp. Grades 2–4.

Lee Ann, a third-grade student in a U.S. school, tells about going every day to an ESL class along with new arrivals from other countries. She enjoys her classes, recess, hot dogs for lunch, and playing video games after school. She and her family also enjoy Vietnamese traditions, especially the celebration of Tet.

The author, a specialist in multicultural education, was a flight attendant on planes that airlifted Vietnamese families to the United States and has often visited Vietnam.

Bunting, Eve. *The Sea World Book of Whales.* Illustrated with photographs from Hubbs Sea World Research Institute. New York & London: Harcourt Brace, 1980. 96 pp. Grades 4–7.

Millions of years ago the ancestors of whales walked on land. This book discusses their evolution, their definition (they are mammals, not fish), the numerous species, their breeding, birth, and development. Whalers and whaling ships are also discussed. The training of killer whales at Sea World in San Diego is described.

Whales have a "language." In 1977, Spaceships *Voyager 1* and *Voyager 2* carried recordings of the songs of humpback whales into space, along with greetings in 55 human languages.

Carter, Jimmy. *Talking Peace: A Vision for the Next Generation.* New York: Dutton Children's Books, 1993. 192 pp. Grade 7 up.

The purpose of this book, written by the 39th president of the United States, is to inform young readers about the possibilities for and the difficulties of achieving peace, good government, and human rights throughout the world. Conflicts of the past and present and efforts to solve problems within nations and among nations are discussed. Homelessness and hunger, in the United States as well as in developing countries, are described.

This book will interest young United States citizens, immigrants, visitors to the United States, and also young residents of other countries.

Caulkins, Janet V. *Pets of the Presidents.* Illustrated with photographs. Brookfield, CT: Milbrook, 1992. 72 pp. Grades 3–6.

President Jefferson liked birds. Lincoln's sons brought goats into the White House, and Theodore Roosevelt's children once smuggled a pony into it. The Roosevelts also had dogs and cats, and Mrs. Roosevelt had a pet snake. The Coolidges had collies, birds, cats, and a raccoon. Franklin D. Roosevelt had a Scottie named Fala. The Kennedys had dogs, horses, ponies, and hamsters. Lyndon Johnson had beagles. Millie, the Bushes' Springer Spaniel, wrote a book, with some help from Mrs. Bush, of course.

This is an entertaining and informative introduction to the presidents of the United States.

Chaikin, Miriam. *Ask Another Question: The Story and Meaning of Passover.* Illustrated by Marvin Friedman. New York: Houghton Mifflin, 1985. 89 pp. Grades 3–6.

When the pharaoh refused to let the Jews leave Egypt, the Angel of Death struck down the Egyptian first-born males. Moses told the Jews to smear the blood of a sacrificial lamb on their doorposts so that the Angel would "pass over" their homes. So began the Feast of the Passover, still celebrated by the Jewish people. In this book their flight from Egypt is described, their wandering in the wilderness, the teachings of Moses, the questions children ask about Passover, and the changes in those questions that reflect later persecutions of the Jews.

————. *Light Another Candle: The Story and Meaning of Hanukkah.* Illustrated by Demi. New York: Houghton Mifflin, 1981. 80 pp. Grades 3–6.

The origin of the celebration of Hanukkah is explained and the customs of its observance are described. Included are a discussion of the Jewish calendar, an explanation of the term BCE, a history of the Temple built by King Solomon, and a description of Jewish foods.

The stylized illustrations in red, white, and black are delicate, tasteful, reverent, and at times humorous.

Donnelly, Judy. *A Wall of Names: The Story of the Vietnam Veterans Memorial.* New York: Random House, 1991. 48 pp. Grades 2–4.

The political causes of the Vietnam War are explained. The decision of the United States to help the South Vietnamese, the escalation of that help, and the reactions of civilian "hawks" and "doves" are presented. Then the story of the memorial conceived by a Vietnam veteran and designed by a young Chinese-American art student is related. Also discussed is the effect the memorial has on the countless people who visit it.

Fisher, Leonard Everett. *Alphabet Art: Thirteen ABCs from around the World.* Illustrated by the author. New York: Macmillan (1978), 1984. 64 pp. Grades 3–7.

An early writing system called *cuneiform* was in use about 3,000 BC in what is now southern Iraq. Its wedge-shaped marks represented either words or syllables. Early Egyptians used picture symbols, called *hieroglyphs*, to represent words, syllables, or ideas. Many modern alphabets and syllabaries have developed from these roots. Others, such as Chinese, have different origins.

The following alphabets and syllabaries are described, illustrated, and discussed: Arabic, Cherokee, Chinese, Cyrillic, Eskimo, Gaelic, German, Greek, Hebrew, Japanese, Sanskrit, Thai, and Tibetan.

————. *The Great Wall of China.* Illustrated by the author. New York: Macmillan, 1986. 32 pp. Grades 1–5.

Over 2,200 years ago, when Mongols were raiding villages in the north of China, the Emperor decreed that a wall should be built to keep the invaders out. It was built by 700,000 workers, with 300,000 soldiers to assure that no one was idle. In 10 years it was finished, and it still stands, although parts have crumbled and had to be repaired.

The double-page black-and-white illustrations are filled with dramatic action. The title on each is in Chinese characters and translated at the back of the book.

Also recommended:

————. *Galileo.* Illustrated by the author. New York: Macmillan, 1992. 28 pp. Grades 2–8.

————. *Pyramid of the Sun, Pyramid of the Moon.* Illustrated by the author. New York: Macmillan, 1988. 30 pp. Grades 1–5.

Fradin, Dennis Brindell. *Remarkable Children: Twenty Who Made History.* Boston & Toronto: Little, Brown, 1987. 207 pp. Grades 4–7.

German, English, French, Spanish, Bedouin, Brazilian, Romanian, Native-American, and Anglo-American children are represented in this collection. Some are well known: Mozart, Louis Braille, Helen Keller, Pablo Picasso, Anne Frank, Shirley Temple, Judy Garland. Others are known by many: Sacajawea, familiar to U.S. school children; John Quincy Adams, who became a U.S. president; Pele, a famous soccer player; Bobby Fischer, chess champion; Cassius Clay, boxer; Tracy Austin, tennis champion. Also included are a child poet, a gymnast, a mathematical prodigy, and young discoverers of cave paintings, the Dead Sea Scrolls, and a comet.

Freedman, Russell. *Lincoln: A Photobiography.* New York: Houghton Mifflin, 1987. 160 pp. Grade 4 up.

The author describes Abraham Lincoln's boyhood, his career as a lawyer, his marriage to Mary Todd, his presidency during the Civil War, and his assassination. The historically accurate and clearly written text modifies some popular legends about Lincoln.

Since the U.S. Civil War was among the earliest wars to be extensively photographed, this pictorial bibliography is especially appropriate.

————. *The Wright Brothers: How They Invented the Airplane.* New York: Holiday House, 1991. Illustrated with photographs by Wilbur & Orville Wright. 128 pp. Grade 5 up.

More than a biography, this book includes information about man's earliest attempts to fly. But the Wright brothers are the central characters, with the emphasis on their mechanical aptitude and their achievements.

The photographs, many of them full page, are as interesting as the text.

Fritz, Jean. *China's Long March: 6,000 Miles of Danger.* Illustrated by Yang Zhr Cheng. New York: Putnam's, 1988. 124 pp. Grade 7 up.

In 1934 the Chinese Nationalist Party, led by Chiang Kai-shek, was at war with the Communists, led by Mao Zedong, who commanded a unit that marched 6,000 miles. Mao's amazing army stretched for 60 miles when marching single file over narrow mountain trails. These men (and some women) crossed the broken bridges over raging rivers, mountains covered with century-old snow, and wastelands of swamps and quicksand. Many died, some in battles, some in crossing the dangerous terrain.

Mao was a remarkable military leader but a ruthless political leader. The survivors of this long march believe the chaotic Cultural Revolution he sponsored from 1966 to 1976 was a mistake.

Giblin, James Cross. *Chimney Sweeps.* Illustrated by Margot Tomes & with photographs. New York: Crowell, 1982. 56 pp. Grades 5–6.

When the Normans conquered England in 1066 they erected castles and tall houses. Flues, or shafts, and then chimneys were constructed to get smoke out of these structures. By the 18th century the flues were so narrow that only small boys could clean them. Sometimes children as young as four were used, under harsh and dangerous conditions.

This sad account has a happy ending. Today, in Europe and the United States, chimneys are cleaned by adults who wear the traditional top hat and tailcoat, use modern equipment, and are well paid.

———. *From Hand to Mouth: Or How We Invented Knives, Forks, Spoons, and Chopsticks and the Table Manners to Go with Them.* Illustrated with photographs, prints, & drawings. New York: Crowell, 1987. 86 pp. Grades 3–7.

Over 100,000 years ago most people ate with their fingers. Many still do, but millions rely on utensils. Knives were invented early, but not used for eating; spoons were the first eating utensils used in Europe. By the Middle Ages people were using knives and spoons, and etiquette books were written. Forks came later.

There are varying theories about the origins of chopsticks, but by 400 BC the Chinese were using them. Their use spread to Vietnam, Korea, and Japan.

Goldstein, Peggy. *Long Is a Dragon: Chinese Writing for Children.* Illustrated by the author. San Francisco: China Books & Periodicals, 1991. 30 pp. Grades 3–7.

The purpose of this book is to teach children how to write Chinese characters. Less ambitious readers will be satisfied with learning how to read a few of them or with simply becoming aware of the Chinese method of writing. Chinese students who can already read the characters may find the book a useful English vocabulary builder.

The illustrations, in red and black, are entertaining as well as helpful.

Graham-Barber, Lynda. *Doodle Dandy: The Complete Book of Independence Day Words.* Illustrated by Betsy Lewin. New York, Oxford, Sydney: Maxwell Macmillan International, 1991. 122 pp. Grades 4–10.

Here is information about Rome, England, France, and Germany, as well as the United States. Among other things, the names of foods traditionally eaten on Independence Day are included. *Hamburger* comes from Germany; *wiener* from Vienna; *mayonnaise* from Mahon, Minora, an island near Spain.

The Declaration of Independence, the Pledge of Allegiance, and the first verse of the "Star-Spangled Banner" are included.

————. *Gobble! The Complete Book of Thanksgiving Words.* Illustrated by Betsy Lewin. New York: Bradbury; Toronto; Collier Macmillan Canada; New York, Oxford, Singapore, Sydney: Maxwell Macmillan International, 1991. 122 pp. Grades 4–10.

Harvest festivals such as Thanksgiving have been, and still are, celebrated throughout the world in countries as different as Germany, Mexico, China, India, and ancient Greece. This book explains the origin and meaning of words related to Thanksgiving in the United States: *Puritan, pilgrim, Mayflower, corn, gobble,* and more. Readers will learn about U.S. history as well as about English words.

Also recommended:

————. *Mushy: The Complete Book of Valentine Words.* Illustrated by Betsy Lewin. New York: Bradbury; Toronto: Collier Macmillan Canada; New York, Oxford, Singapore, Sydney: Maxwell Macmillan International, 1991. 122 pp. Grades 4–10.

Greene, Carol. *Holidays around the World.* Illustrated with color photographs from various sources. Chicago: Childrens Press, 1982. 30 pp. K–4.

Just about every kind of holiday is mentioned. There are private holidays such as birthdays and anniversaries, special days in history, such as Australia Day, and days for special people: St. Patrick's Day in Ireland, Mother's Day in the United States, and Children's Day in Japan. Religious holidays include Jewish, Buddhist, Hindu, Muslim, Christian, and more.

————. *Marco Polo: Voyager to the Orient.* Illustrated with black-and-white pictures from Historical Picture Services. Chicago: Childrens Press, 1987. 99 pp. Grade 4 up.

The adventures of the world's most famous traveler, a native of Venice, make exciting reading. This book is also a good vocabulary builder, as the author defines and gives the origin of words such as *turquoise* (Turkish Stone), *Tartars* (from Greek *Tartar*, meaning hell), *gauze* (from the city of Gouza), *pacific* (peaceful), and *probity* (honesty).

Hamilton, Virginia. *In the Beginning: Creation Stories from around the World.* Illustrated by Barry Moser. San Diego, New York, London; Harcourt Brace Jovanovich, 1988. 157 pp. PS up.

Myths are defined as stories about events that caused changes. Included in this book are Eskimo myths, Native-American myths, and myths from Pacific islands, China, Australia, Israel, Iceland, Babylon, Greece, Russia, Guatemala, and countries on the African continent. Some readers will recognize Ananse the Spider, featured in African myths. Some will be familiar with the two stories from the Old Testament, and some will recognize Greek myths.

————. *Many Thousand Gone: African Americans from Slavery to Freedom.* Illustrated by Leo & Diane Dillon. New York: Knopf; Toronto: Random House of Canada, 1993. 151 pp. Grade 4 up.

The first Africans brought to the American colonies had been stolen from their homes by slave traders, brought by a Dutch ship to Virginia, and traded to that colony for food and other supplies. They were made indentured servants. By 1660 Virginia and Maryland had made Black servants slaves for life.

This book tells of those who escaped to the north, or tried to, and of those who returned to help others escape through the "underground railroad." Each chapter tells of the suffering, torture, and courage of a slave, of the cruelty of the slave owners, and of the courage of those, Black and White, who helped the "runningaways."

Hewett, Joan. *Hector Lives in the United States Now: The Story of a Mexican-American Child.* New York: Lippincott, 1990. 44 pp. Grades 2–5.

Ten-year-old Hector lives in Los Angeles with his parents and three younger brothers. Born in Guadalajara, Mexico, Hector and 9-year-old Polo are Mexican citizens. Like their parents, they have temporary legal-resident cards that permit them to go to Mexico and return to the United States, and they look forward to visiting relatives there. The two younger boys, born in the United States, are citizens. The father, mother, Hector, and Polo will become naturalized citizens soon.

Hector plays soccer, basketball, and volleyball. He and Polo speak English and Spanish, and Hector, as the oldest child, is the family spokesperson.

Hoyt-Goldsmith, Diane. *Pueblo Storyteller.* Illustrated with color photographs by Lawrence Migdale. New York: Holiday House, 1991. 26 pp. Grades 3–6.

April, a Pueblo girl, describes her life as a child of two cultures. She rides to school in a modern bus and plays "Twinkle, Twinkle, Little Star" on a saxophone. She also bakes bread in a Pueblo oven, eats Pueblo foods, and makes pottery. Her grandparents tell her stories about their past and legends of their people.

The bright-colored photographs show April, her family, and her friends playing golf and basketball as well as engaging in Pueblo activities, such as the Buffalo dance.

Huynh Quang Nhuong. *The Land I Lost: Adventures of a Boy in Vietnam.* Illustrated by Vo-Dinh Mai. Cambridge, Philadelphia, San Francisco, London, Mexico City, São Paulo, Sydney: Harper & Row, 1982. 115 pp. Grades 4–7.

This unique memoir begins with the acquisition by the author's family of a water buffalo that becomes a courageous and loyal pet, and ends with its death. Appropriately named Tank, the buffalo seems invincible as well as intelligent, but he is killed by a bullet shot in the fighting between the French forces and the Resistance.

Although Tank is the central figure, there are stories about monkeys, a crocodile, snakes, birds, chickens, a wild hog, and more wild life, as well as about the author's family.

Jacobs, Francine. *The Tainos: The People Who Welcomed Columbus.* Illustrated by Patrick Collins. New York: Putnam's, 1992. 107 pp. Grades 5–9.

The gentle natives of the Caribbean were captured, enslaved, and brutalized by the Spaniards who arrived with Columbus in 1492. Within 50 years they were practically wiped out, and today the West Indies are inhabited mostly by people of European and African descent.

Because this book is so tightly packed with information and filled with accounts of cruelty, it is not easy to read, but it is well worth the trouble.

Jacobs, William J. *Ellis Island: New Hope in a New Land.* Illustrated with black-and-white photographs from varied sources. New York: Scribner's, 1990. 34 pp. Grades 2–5.

This brief but inspiring account of how America has been populated by "newcomers" begins with so-called Indians, who walked across what was once a land bridge from Asia to Alaska. It ends with recent arrivals from the west and south. Much of the text is about Europeans who arrived at Ellis Island; almost all of the photographs show New York City and its harbor.

Kelley, Emily. *Christmas around the World.* Illustrated by Priscilla Kiedrowski. Minneapolis: Carolrhoda, 1986. 48 pp. K–4.

The religious aspects of Christmas are emphasized: in Iran, where the three wise men lived; in Sweden, where Christmastime begins on St. Lucia Day, December 13; in Iraq, where on Christmas Eve a child reads about the birth of Jesus; in Spain, where Twelfth Night (January 6) is celebrated; in Norway, where most families go to church. In China, Santa Claus comes to fill children's stockings, as he does in many other countries.

Cheerful, brightly drawn colored illustrations alternate with black-and-white drawings, all showing the happiness of people observing this holiday.

———. *Happy New Year.* Illustrated by Priscilla Kiedrowski. Minneapolis: Carolrhoda, 1984. 48 pp. K–4.

In the United States and in many other places New Year's Day is celebrated on January 1. In Iran the New Year begins on March 20 and is celebrated for thirteen days. The Jewish New Year, called Rosh Hashanah, lasts for 1 or 2 days, usually in September. In Vietnam, New Year's is called Tet. It begins between January 21 and February 19. The Mandingo people of Sierra Leone celebrate it in March or April. Chinese New Year is in January or February. Various ways of celebrating this holiday are described.

Lively, colorful illustrations depict the setting, clothing, and activities typical of each culture.

Also recommended:

———. *April Fool's Day.* Illustrated by C. A. Nobens. Minneapolis: Carolrhoda, 1983. 56 pp. K–4.

Kent, Zachary. *The Story of the Saigon Airlift.* Illustrated with photographs. Chicago: Childrens Press, 1991. 32 pp. Grades 3–8.

In April 1975 the United States was forced to end a 10-year-long attempt to defeat the Viet Cong and save South Vietnam from communism. Thousands of Vietnamese were evacuated by air and flown to the United States. The U.S. Navy rescued 60,000 more from rafts, fishing boats, and cargo ships in the South China Sea. In May 1975 the refugees—many of them doctors, lawyers, engineers, and teachers—reached the United States. Since then more Southeast Asians have arrived. In spite of the hardships and difficulties in adjusting to their new home, many now hold responsible positions.

Le Tord, Bijou, compiler. *Peace on Earth: A Book of Prayers from Around the World.* Illustrated by the compiler. New York: Doubleday, 1992. 80 pp. All ages.

Here are prayers about morning, night, the sun, the moon, plants, children, animals, and more. Many are by Native Americans. There are prayers from England, Holland, Mexico, India, Israel, Japan, Pakistan, Wales, Italy, Ecuador, Greece, and African countries. Some are by famous poets, some are by saints, and some are by children.

The delicate watercolor illustrations show earth, sky, and water, with people and animals.

Limburg, Peter R. *Weird: The Complete Book of Halloween Words.* Illustrated by Betsy Lewin. New York: Macmillan, 1989. 122 pp. Grades 4–10.

This book about the origin of words such as *ghost, witch,* and *weird* is sprinkled with tidbits of history, literature, social customs, and mythology. Included are a historical time line, a list of suggestions for additional reading, a bibliography of the author's sources, and an index. The humorous India ink drawings enliven the text.

McGuire, William. *Southeast Asians.* Illustrated with photographs, most in color. New York, London, Toronto, Sydney: Franklin Watts, 1991. 64 pp. Grades 5–10.

Between 1975 and 1984, refugees came to the United States from Vietnam, Laos, and Cambodia. Many had fled in boats to refugee camps, where they were given orientation and English language classes and sometimes money when they left. Eventually, many refugees reached the United States; others went to Hong Kong, Canada, Europe, and Australia. Many have had problems adjusting, but most have done well, especially the young people attending U.S. schools.

Meltzer, Milton. *The Chinese Americans.* Illustrated with photographs. New York: Crowell, 1980. 181 pp. Grade 5 up.

Chinese immigrants who came to the United States in the 19th century worked on the Union Pacific Railroad, mined gold, farmed, and fished. They were hard workers, but underpaid and mistreated. Slowly, the discrimination lessened. In 1952 they were no longer barred from owning land in California, and in 1964 the Civil Rights Act barred discrimination in employment.

The author expresses admiration for the Chinese and impatience with the Americans who mistreated them.

————. *Hispanic Americans.* Illustrated with photographs. New York: Crowell, 1982. 149 pp. Grade 5 up.

The Spanish were the first Europeans to settle in the New World (North America, South America, Central America, Mexico, and the islands of the Caribbean). They interbred with Indians, Blacks, and Anglos (Whites). Called Hispanics because of their language, these peoples have been mistreated, according to the author, by those who came from northern Europe.

Also recommended:

————. *Columbus and the World around Him.* New York: Franklin Watts, 1990. 192 pp. Grade 6 up.

————. *George Washington and the Birth of Our Nation.* Illustrated with photographs of paintings and engravings and with maps. New York, London, Toronto, Sydney: Franklin Watts, 1986. 176 pp. Grade 7 up.

Mitchell, Barbara. *Between Two Worlds: A Story About Pearl Buck.* Illustrated by Karen Ritz. Minneapolis: Carolrhoda, 1988. 64 pp. Grades 3–6.

Pearl Buck (1892–1973) spent her early childhood in China, where her parents were missionaries. When she was 10 years old she went to West Virginia, where she met relatives and realized that she belonged to two worlds: China and the United States. She spent much of her life in China, but eventually settled in the United States. In 1931 her best-known novel, *The Good Earth,* set in China, was published. She wrote books for children as well as for adults.

Morey, Janet Nomura, & Dunn, Wendy. *Famous Asian Americans.* Illustrated with photographs. New York: Dutton, 1992. 170 pp. Grade 5 up.

Except for Ellison S. Onizuka, who was on the *Challenger* flight that ended in tragedy in 1986, the 14 people in this collective biography were still alive when the book was published. Included are men and women in various fields: art, literature, engineering, journalism, music, business, acting, medicine, law, sports, politics, physics, and architecture. All are Asian Americans, but their ethnic backgrounds are varied: Filipino, Chinese, Korean, Japanese, Cambodian, Vietnamese.

Myers, Walter Dean. *Malcolm X: By Any Means Possible.* New York: Scholastic, 1993. 210 pp. Grade 7 up.

Although he was bright and did well in school, Malcolm Little was discouraged, because he was Black, from making use of his intelligence. In his teens he became a "hustler" in Harlem and spent 6 years in prison, where he became interested in the Nation of Islam religion. After his release he became a member, changing his name to Malcolm X, and then a minister. He encouraged hatred of White people, but after making a pilgrimage to Mecca he left the Nation of Islam. He was building the Organization of Afro-American Unity when he was assassinated.

His impelling story is told against the turbulent background of the Civil Rights Movement of the 1960s.

Patterson, Lillie. *Martin Luther King, Jr., and the Freedom Movement.* New York: Facts on File, 1989. 178 pp. Grade 7 up.

After the Montgomery, Alabama, bus boycott was started in 1955, Martin Luther King became the leader of the Civil Rights Movement. He was arrested countless times in his efforts to eliminate segregation. He is remembered for his "I Have a Dream" speech made in Washington in 1963; for the march on Selma, Alabama, that he led in 1965; and much more. He was assassinated in Memphis, Tennessee, on April 3, 1968.

Other events of the 1960s that protested the segregation of Blacks were the integration of Central High School in Little Rock, Arkansas; the sit-ins at lunch counters that refused to serve Blacks; and the Freedom Rides in interstate buses. All these and more are discussed in this biography.

Pelta, Kathy. *Discovering Christopher Columbus: How History Is Invented.* Illustrated with maps, portraits, and photographs of objects and places from various sources. Minneapolis: Lerner, 1991. 112 pp. Grades 4–6.

This book is more than a biography. It traces, century by century, differing accounts of Columbus's life; his trips to the "New World"; the places that have been named for him; the methods historians have used in uncovering material about him; the controversies about his life, his personality, his character, and his accomplishments. The last chapter, "You the Historian," includes an annotated bibliography.

The illustrations, as well as the book, are worth careful study.

Perl, Lila. *Blue Monday and Friday the Thirteenth: The Stories behind the Days of the Week.* Illustrated by Erika Weihs. New York: Houghton Mifflin, 1986. 96 pp. Grades 3–6.

There is no scientific reason for the 7-day week, which probably began in Babylonia over 4,000 years ago. The Chinese week once included 60 days and then was broken up into 10-day weeks. Now it has 7 days.

The names of days in Romance languages are similar. The Latin word for moon is *luna*; so in French, Monday is *lundi*. English, a Germanic language, is similar to German, in which Monday is *Montag*, and Norwegian, in which it is *mandag*. There are many other interesting etymological similarities.

————. *Candles, Cakes, and Donkey Tails: Birthday Symbols and Celebrations.* Illustrated by Victoria de Larrea. New York: Houghton Mifflin, 1984. 71 pp. Grades 3–6.

Birthdates of important people, such as generals and national heroes, were celebrated long ago. Ordinary people began to celebrate birthdays in more recent times. Some people believe that character is influenced by the sign of the zodiac (whether Western or Chinese) under which one is born.

In Western countries candles and cakes are symbolic of birthday parties, as are certain games. Name days and coming-of-age ceremonies are also important in many cultures.

Pinchot, Jane. *The Mexicans in America.* Illustrated with historic black-and-white photographs from various sources. Minneapolis: Lerner (1973), 1989 (rev. ed.). 99 pp. Grade 5 up.

The history of Mexican Americans is covered from the time the Spaniards arrived in the 16th century. The early civilization of the Aztec empire is described with respect and admiration. The claims of France, Russia, and Great Britain in the 18th and 19th centuries, the settlements of Anglo-Americans that began in 1821, and the constant struggle of the Mexicans, with their shared Indian-Spanish heritage, against the oppressive "Anglos," are discussed. The achievements of Mexican Americans in politics, scholarship, sports, and the arts are noted in this stimulating account.

Ride, Sally. *Voyager: An Adventure to the Edge of the Solar System.* Illustrated with photographs from NASA. New York: Crown, 1992. 36 pp. Grades 2–5.

In 1977 two spacecraft, *Voyager 1* and *Voyager 2*, were launched from Earth to explore Jupiter, Saturn, Uranus, and Neptune. Unmanned, they are still traveling and collecting data but no longer taking pictures. In case either one is found by space travelers from another world, they carry pictures and sounds from Earth.

Ride, Sally, with Susan Okie. *To Space and Back.* Illustrated with color photographs. New York: Lothrop, 1989. 96 pp. Grade 1 up.

The author describes her personal experience in space travel, covering the way in which astronauts eat, sleep, and work, and the effects of weightlessness. The striking photographs and the readable, sometimes humorous, text make this book exciting as well as informative.

Rodari, Florian. *A Weekend with Picasso.* Translation of *Un dimanche avec Picasso.* Illustrated with photographs of the artist, his studio, the subjects of his paintings, his works, and the works of other great artists. New York: Rizzoli International, 1991. 64 pp. Grades 3–6.

Written as if by Pablo Picasso himself, the text explains his method, his paintings, and the philosophy behind his art. On this amusing excursion readers will enjoy Picasso's love of life and sense of humor while developing an appreciation for and an understanding of his work. Museums where his art can be seen are listed at the end. Important dates in his life (1881–1971) are also included.

Sarnoff, Jane. *Words: A Book about the Origins of Everyday Words and Phrases.* Illustrated by Reynold Ruffins. New York: Scribner's, 1981. 64 pp. Grades 4–8.

The history of the English language is summarized in a few pages, followed by entertaining stories about some ordinary English words. They are classified according to subjects: the family, ships at sea, friends and enemies, clothes, and 10 other topics. Fewer than 200 words are discussed, but the discussions are entertaining as well as informative. A list of about 70 proper names with their meaning and/or origin is included.

Say, Allen. *El Chino.* Illustrated by the author. Boston: Houghton Mifflin, 1990. 32 pp. Grades 2–6.

All Bill Wong wanted to do was play basketball, and he was good at it. But he was too short to play in college, where he studied engineering. He became an engineer, and on his first vacation he went to Spain, saw a bullfighter shorter than he was, and decided to go to bullfighting school. The other students said that he could not become a matador because he wasn't Spanish, but he proved them wrong.

Schwartz, David M. *How Much Is a Million?* Illustrated by Steven Kellogg. New York: Lothrop, 1985. 36 pp. K–5.

In addition to giving children a minilesson in mathematics, this book offers English language learners of any age excellent examples of the use of the conditional, as in "If you wanted to count from 1 to 1 million, it would take you about 23 days." It also answers the questions *How big is a billion?* and *How big is a trillion?*

The large (mostly full-page) watercolor illustrations, in subdued shades, capture the book's amazing mathematical concepts as explained by Marvelosissimo the Mathematical Magician.

————. *If You Made a Million.* Illustrated by Steven Kellogg. New York: Lothrop, 1989. 40 pp. Grades 2–5.

Marvelosissimo the Mathematical Magician leads his little workers through the process of earning and spending money, from 1 cent (earn it by feeding a fish, spend it for a pebble) to 1 million dollars (earn it by taming an obstreperous ogre, spend it on real estate for endangered rhinoceroses). The book ends with that perennial question: What would you do if you made a million dollars?

The illustrations are colorful and imaginative.

Simon, Seymour. *Space Words: A Dictionary.* Illustrated by Randy Chewning. New York: HarperCollins, 1991. 48 pp. Grades 2–5.

This readable, illustrated dictionary begins with *Apollo Program* and ends with *zodiac.* It includes people (Nicolaus Copernicus, Albert Einstein) as well as phenomena (Halley's comet, phases of the moon), objects (space suit, meteorite, space shuttle), and more. The definitions are brief and clear. The illustrations are vivid, spectacular, and meaningful.

————. *The Sun.* Illustrated with color photographs, most from NASA. New York: Mulberry Books, 1986. 28 pp. K–3.

The sun is large enough to hold 1.3 million Earths. It is comparable to an endless hydrogen bomb, with temperatures that may reach 27 million degrees at its core. Giant storms, called sunspots, erupt on its surface and send electrical energy into space.

The importance of the sun to life on earth is emphasized, as well as its size and power.

Also recommended:

————. *Stars.* Illustrated with large color photographs from several sources. New York: William Morrow, 1986. 28 pp. PS–3.

Sinnott, Susan. *Extraordinary Hispanic Americans.* Illustrated with photographs. Chicago: Childrens Press, 1991. 277 pp. Grade 4 up.

Suitable for browsing and for reference, this comprehensive collection of brief biographies begins with Columbus and ends with a woman astronaut from California and a young boxer from Arizona. Included are explorers, settlers, missionaries, writers, actors, artists, musicians, political activists, and more. There are quite a few surprises. Linda Ronstadt, for example, is of Hispanic as well as German descent. And Pablo Casals, the famous cellist, left Spain while Franco was in power and eventually settled in Puerto Rico, the birthplace of his mother.

Skira-Venturi, Rosabianca. *A Weekend with Degas.* Translation of *Un dimanche avec Degas.* Illustrated with reproductions of works by Degas and his friends and with photographs. New York: Rizzoli International, 1991. 62 pp. Grades 3–6.

In addition to many of his own famous paintings, works by friends of Degas, photographs of Paris, lithographs, and engravings illustrate this revealing account, written as if by Degas himself. Many of his famous paintings of ballet dancers are included, along with racetrack scenes, musicians, and more.

Stanley, Fay. *The Last Princess: The Story of Princess Ka'iulani of Hawai'i.* Illustrated by Diane Stanley. New York: Four Winds. Toronto: Collier Macmillan. New York, Oxford, Singapore, Sydney: Maxwell Macmillan International, 1991. 40 pp. Grades 3–6.

In preparation for the future duties she was expected to have as the ruling monarch of the Kingdom of Hawaii, the young princess was educated in England. Born in 1875, she left home before she was 14 and took the long trip to London. In 1893 the United States took control of Hawaii, deposing her aunt, Queen Liliuokalani. The princess tried to persuade President Grover Cleveland to block Hawaii's annexation, but he was unable to do so. Ka'iulani returned to Hawaii, where she died in 1899.

This is a moving account of the annexation to the United States, as a territory, of a tiny island kingdom in the Pacific.

Terban, Marvin. *I Think I Thought and Other Tricky Verbs.* Illustrated by Giulio Maestro. New York: Houghton Mifflin, 1984. 64 pp. PS–4.

Twenty-nine irregular verbs are illustrated with delightfully ridiculous sentences, generous doses of alliteration, and wildly funny illustrations. For example, *Tina teaches turtles not to stumble* is followed by *Talbot taught tigers to toss and tumble.* Three turtles, watched by a duck, are walking a tightrope; on the opposite page four tumbling tigers are skillfully tossing balls.

————. *Your Foot's on My Feet! and Other Tricky Nouns.* Illustrated by Giulio Maestro. New York: Houghton Mifflin, 1986. 62 pp. Grades 2–5.

Nouns are classified as those that form plurals by changing their endings (*boys, children, babies*), those that change in the middle (*feet, mice*), those that don't change at all (*deer, moose*), and those that have more than one plural (*fish* or *fishes, scarfs* or *scarves*), and finally some "irregular irregular" nouns (*scissors, scissors; mongoose, mongooses*).

All examples are illustrated with clever rhymes and pictures.

Also recommended: Terban's other delightfully humorous books about English words, idioms, pronunciation, and origins.

Thomson, Peggy. *City Kids in China.* Illustrated with photographs by Paul S. Conklin. New York: HarperCollins, 1991. 114 pp. Grades 3–7.

In this refreshingly cheerful book about China, the children of Changsha study, ride bicycles, dance, play violin and cello, read comic books, jump rope, play Ping-Pong, hopscotch, cards, and more. In text and photographs most are shown as happy, some as serious, none as sad. Sprinkled throughout the book are little essays written, in English, by school children.

Uchida, Yoshiko. *The Invisible Thread.* Illustrated with photographs of the author and her family. Englewood Cliffs, NJ: Simon & Schuster, 1991. 136 pp. Grade 7 up.

This dramatic memoir by a well-known Japanese-American author of children's books will appeal to young people who have read her novels, especially *A Jar of Dreams, The Best Bad Thing*, and *The Happiest Ending.* It tells of cultural, social, and economic problems that she and her family faced, their life in an internment camp during World War II, her education at the University of California and at Smith College, her first job as a teacher, and her goals and achievements as a writer.

Williams, Terry Tempest, & Major, Ted. *The Secret Language of Snow.* Illustrated by Jennifer Dewey. San Francisco & New York: Sierra Club/ Pantheon Books, 1984. 129 pp. Grades 3–7.

Some basic structural types of snow crystals are described. Eskimo words for 10 kinds of snow (for example, *anui* for falling snow, *pukak* for snow that can cause avalanches, *siqoq* for swirling or drifting snow) are defined. Hibernation and other adaptations to winter are explained. The dangers, as well as the uses, of snow are included. For example, snow that acts as an insulating blanket for small mammals also causes avalanches.

Willson, Robina Beckles. *Merry Christmas! Children at Christmastime around the World.* Illustrated by Satomi Ichikawa. New York: Putnam's, 1983. 74 pp. K up.

The story of the Nativity is followed by a brief account of animal legends related to Christmas. The rest of the book describes Christmas customs in Great Britain, the United States, Germany, the Netherlands, Poland and Czechoslovakia, Finland, Sweden, Russia, France, Italy, Greece, Mexico, India, Japan, and Australia. Also included are carols, recipes, and directions for making ornaments.

The illustrations show children in each country engaged in activities typical of their culture.

Appendix A

Cross Reference: Location and Ethnic Background

Roman numerals indicate the section in which the entry can be found.

Africa

(See also *Egypt, Ethiopia, and the Middle East.*)

Aardema, V.	*Anansi Finds a Fool*, II
	Oh Kojo! How Could You! (Ashanti), II
	Traveling to Tondo (Zaire), II
	Who's in Rabbit's House? (Masai), II
French, F.	*Anancy and Mr. Dry-Bone*, II
Naidoo, B.	*Chain of Fire* (South Africa), III
	Journey to Jo'burg (South Africa), III
Sacks, M.	*Beyond Safe Boundaries* (South Africa), III
Steptoe, J.	*Mufaro's Beautiful Daughters* (Zimbabwe), II

African Americans

Berleth, R.	*Samuel's Choice*, III
Hamilton, V.	*The House of Dies Drear*, III
	Many Thousand Gone, IV
	Mystery of Drear House, III
Myers, W. D.	*Malcolm X*, IV
	Me, Mop, and the Moondance Kid, III
	Mop, Moondance, and the Nagasaki Knights, III
Patterson, L.	*Martin Luther King, Jr. and the Freedom Movement*, IV
Polacco, P.	*Mrs. Katz and Tush*, I
Say, A.	*The Bicycle Man*, I

Asia

Baillie, A.	*Little Brother* (Cambodia), III
Blumberg, R.	*Commodore Perry in the Land of the Shogun* (Japan), IV

Buck, P. S.	*The Big Wave* (Japan), III
Choi, S. N.	*Year of Impossible Goodbyes* (Korea), III
Climo, S.	*The Korean Cinderella*, II
Compton, P.	*The Terrible Eek* (Japan), II
Day, D.	*The Sleeper* (China), II
Demi	*Chen Ping and His Magic Axe* (China), II
	The Empty Pot (China), II
	Liang and the Magic Paintbrush (China), II
	The Magic Boat (China), II
Fisher, L. E.	*The Great Wall of China*, IV
Flack, M.	*The Story about Ping* (China), I
Fritz, J.	*China's Long March*, IV
Ginsberg, M.	*The Chinese Mirror* (Korea), II
Godden, R.	*The Valiant Chatti-maker* (India), III
Goldstein, P.	*Long Is a Dragon* (Chinese writing), IV
Haugaard, E. C.	*The Boy and the Samurai* (Japan), III
	The Samurai's Tale (Japan), III
Ho, M.	*The Clay Marble* (Cambodia), III
	Rice Without Rain (Thailand), III
Hong, L. T.	*How the Ox Star Fell from Heaven* (China), II
Huynh Quang Nhuong	*The Land I Lost: Adventures of a Boy in Vietnam*, IV
Kent, Z.	*The Story of the Saigon Airlift* (Vietnam), IV
Mitchell, B.	*Between Two Worlds* (China and the United States), IV
Namioka, L.	*The Coming of the Bear* (Japan), III
Newton, P.	*The Stonecutter* (India), II
Paterson, K.	*The Master Puppeteer* (Japan), III
	Rebels of the Heavenly Kingdom (China), III
	The Sign of the Chrysanthemum (Japan), III
Sakade, F.	*Japanese Children's Favorite Stories*, I
Say, A.	*The Bicycle Man* (Japan), I
	The Inn-Keeper's Apprentice (Japan), III
Schlein, M.	*The Year of the Panda* (China), III
Tejima, K.	*Ho-Limlim* (Japan), II
Thomson, P.	*City Kids in China*, IV
Tompert, A.	*Grandfather Tang's Story* (China), I
Wallace, I.	*Chin Chiang and the Dragon's Dance* (China), I
Wang, R. C.	*The Fourth Question* (China), II

Watkins, Y. K.	*So Far from the Bamboo Grove* (Japanese in Korea), III
	Tales from the Bamboo Grove (Korea), II
Whelan, G.	*Goodbye, Vietnam*, III
Yacowitz, C.	*The Jade Stone* (China), II
Yashima, T.	*Umbrella* (Japan), I
Yen, C.	*Why Rat Comes First* (China), II
Yolen, J.	*The Seeing Stick* (China), II
Young, E.	*Lon Po Po* (China), II

Asians in Canada, Europe, and the United States

Baker, C. G.	*Fight for Honor* and sequels (Vietnamese in the United States), III
Breckler, R.	*Hoang Breaks the Magic Teapot* (Vietnamese in the United States), II
Brown, T.	*Lee Ann* (Vietnamese in the United States), IV
Crew, L.	*Children of the River* (Cambodians in Oregon), III
Garrigue, S.	*The Eternal Spring of Mr. Ito* (Japanese in Canada), III
Godden, R.	*Fu-Dog* (Chinese in London), I
	Little Plum (Japanese dolls in England), I
	Miss Happiness and Miss Flower (Japanese dolls in England), I
Irwin, H.	*Kim/Kimi* (Japanese Americans in California), III
Lord, B. B.	*In the Year of the Boar and Jackie Robinson* (Chinese in the United States), III
McGuire, W.	*Southeast Asians* (refugees), IV
Meltzer, M.	*The Chinese Americans*, IV
Morey, J. N., & Dunn, W.	*Famous Asian Americans*, IV
Myers, W. D.	*Mop, Moondance, and the Nagasaki Knights* (Japanese children's baseball team in the United States), III
Namioka, L.	*Yang the Youngest and His Terrible Ear* (Chinese in Seattle), III
Say, A.	*El Chino* (Chinese American in Spain), IV
Uchida, Y.	*The Invisible Thread* (Japanese Americans), IV
	A Jar of Dreams and sequels (Japanese in California), III
Yee, P.	*Tales from Gold Mountain* (Chinese in Canada and the United States), I
Yep, L.	*The Star Fisher* (Chinese in the United States), III

Egypt, Ethiopia, and the Middle East

Carter, D. S.	*His Majesty, Queen Hatshepsut* (Egypt), III
Chaikin, M.	*Ask Another Question* (Egypt), IV
	Light Another Candle (Jerusalem), IV
Climo, S.	*The Egyptian Cinderella*, II
Heide, F. P., & Gilliland, J. H.	*The Day of Ahmed's Secret* (Cairo), I
	Sami and the Time of Troubles (Beirut), I
Laird, E.	*The Road to Bethlehem* (Ethiopia), II
Menotti, G. C.	*Amahl and the Night Visitors* (Palestine), III

Europe

Allen, L.	*The Giant Who Had No Heart*, II
	The Mouse Bride (Finland), II
Anno, M.	*Anno's Journey* (northern Europe), I
Banks, L. R.	*The Indian in the Cupboard* and sequels (England), III
Dahl, R.	*Esio Trot* (England), III
	Matilda (England), III
	Minpins (England), II
De Gerez, T.	*Louhi, Witch of North Farm* (Finland), II
De Paola, T.	*Tony's Bread* (Italy), II
Fisher, L. E.	*Galileo* (Italy), IV
Giblin, J. C.	*Chimney Sweeps* (London), IV
Greene, J. D.	*What His Father Did* (Russia), II
Haugaard, E. C.	*Prince Boghole* (Ireland), II
Hendry, D.	*A Camel Called April* (England), I
	Christmas on Exeter Street (England), I
	The Not-Anywhere House (England), I
Hesse, K.	*Letters from Rifka* (Russian emigrants), III
Johnston, N.	*The Delphic Choice* (Greece and Turkey), III
Kirstein, L.	*Puss in Boots*, II
Lagerlof, S.	*The Changeling* (Sweden), II
Leaf, M.	*The Story of Ferdinand* (Spain), I
Lowry, L.	*Number the Stars* (Denmark), III
Mayer, M.	*The Prince and the Princess* (Bohemia), II
	The Sorcerer's Apprentice (Greece), II
Morpurgo, M.	*Waiting for Anya* (France), III
Paterson, K.	*The King's Equal*, II
Rodari, F.	*A Weekend with Picasso* (Spain, France), IV

Skira-Venturi, R.   *A Weekend with Degas* (France), IV
Winthrop, E.   *Vasilissa the Beautiful* (Russia), II

Hispanics

Aardema, V.   *Pedro and the Padre* (Mexico), II
Belpré, P.   *Perez and Martina* (Puerto Rico), II
Brusca, M.   *On the Pampas* (Argentina), I
Dorros, A.   *Abuela* (New York City), I
Fisher, L. E.   *Pyramid of the Sun, Pyramid of the Moon* (Mexico), IV
Hewett, J.   *Hector Lives in the United States Now* (Los Angeles), IV
    Laura Loves Horses (California), I
Krumbold, J.   *. . . and now Miguel* (New Mexico), III
Meltzer, M.   *Hispanic Americans*, IV
Neugeboren, J.   *Poli* (Texas), III
Pinchot, J.   *The Mexicans in America*, IV
Sinnott, S.   *Extraordinary Hispanic Americans*, IV
Tompert, A.   *The Silver Whistle* (southwestern United States), I
Weiss, N.   *On a Hot, Hot Day* (southwestern United States), I

Islands, Oceans, and Explorers

Blumberg, R.   *The Remarkable Voyages of Captain Cook* (Pacific Ocean), IV
Bryan, A.   *The Cat's Purr* (West Indies), II
    Turtle Knows Your Name (West Indies), II
Conrad, P.   *Pedro's Journal* (Caribbean), III
Dorris, M.   *Morning Girl* (Caribbean), III
French, F.   *Anancy and Mr. Dry-Bone* (Jamaica), II
Jacobs, F.   *The Tainos* (Caribbean), IV
Meltzer, M.   *Columbus and the World around Him*, IV
O'Dell, S.   *Island of the Blue Dolphins* (Pacific), III
    My Name Is Not Angelica (West Indies), III
    Zia (Pacific), III
Pelta, K.   *Discovering Christopher Columbus*, IV
Stanley, F.   *The Last Princess* (Hawaii), IV

Native Americans and Eskimos

Andrews, J.   *The Very Last First Time* (Inuits in northern Canada), I
Banks, L. R.   *The Indian in the Cupboard* and sequels, III

Batherman, M.	*Before Columbus*, IV
De Paola, T.	*The Legend of the Bluebonnet*, II *The Legend of the Indian Paintbrush*, II
Dorris, M.	*Morning Girl* (Tainos), III
Esbensen, B. J.	*Ladder to the Sky* (Ojibway), II
Goble, P.	*Crow Chief* (Plains Indian), II *The Great Race of the Birds and Animals* (Cheyenne and Sioux), II
Hoyt-Goldsmith, D.	*Pueblo Storyteller*, IV
Jacobs, F.	*The Tainos*, IV
Loverseed, A.	*Tikkatoo's Journey* (Eskimo), II
Neugeboren, J.	*Poli* (Comanche), III
O'Dell, S.	*Island of the Blue Dolphins*, III *Zia*, III
Oughton, J.	*How the Stars Fell into the Sky* (Navajo), II
Van Laan, N.	*Rainbow Crow* (Lenape), II
Williams, T. T., & Major, T.	*The Secret Language of Snow* (Eskimo), IV

United States

(See also *African Americans* and *Asians in the United States, Canada, and Europe*.)

Anno, M.	*Anno's USA*, I
Ashabranner, B.	*Always to Remember* (Washington, DC), IV
Blume, J.	*Tales of a Fourth Grade Nothing* and sequels, III
Caulkins, J. V.	*Pets of the Presidents* (Washington, DC), IV
Cleary, B.	*The Mouse and the Motorcycle* and sequels (California), III *Muggie Maggie*, III
Cormier, R.	*Tunes for Bears to Dance To*, III
Donnelly, J.	*A Wall of Names* (Washington, DC), IV
Ernst, L. C.	*Ginger Jumps*, I *Nattie Parsons' Good-Luck Lamb*, I *Sam Johnson and the Blue-Ribbon Quilt*, I *Walter's Tail*, I
Estes, E.	*The Hundred Dresses* (Polish girl in the United States), III
Freedman, R.	*Lincoln*, IV *The Wright Brothers*, IV
Freeman, L. & D.	*Pet of the Met* (New York City), I

George, J. C.	*My Side of the Mountain* (New York State), III
	On the Far Side of the Mountain (New York State), III
Griffin, P. R.	*Otto from Otherwhere* (San Antonio), III
Jacobs, W. J.	*Ellis Island* (New York harbor), IV
Meltzer, M.	*George Washington and the Birth of Our Nation*, IV
Mitchell, B.	*Between Two Worlds* (Pearl Buck), IV
Stolz, M.	*King Emmett the Second* (Ohio), III
Yolen, J.	*All Those Secrets of the World*, I

The World and Beyond
(See also Appendix B, *Holidays and Special Occasions*.)

Branley, F. M.	*Neptune*, IV
Carter, J.	*Talking Peace*, IV
Fisher, L. E.	*Alphabet Art*, IV
Fradin, D. B.	*Remarkable Children*, IV
Giblin, J. C.	*From Hand to Mouth*, IV
Greene, C.	*Holidays around the World*, IV
	Marco Polo, IV
Griffin, P. R.	*Otto from Otherwhere*, III
Hamilton, V.	*In the Beginning*, IV
Kelley, E.	*Christmas around the World*, IV
Kherdian, D.	*Feathers and Tails*, II
Knight, M. B.	*Talking Walls*, I
Le Tord, B.	*Peace on Earth*, IV
Meltzer, M.	*Columbus and the World around Him*, IV
Ride, S.	*To Space and Back*, IV
	Voyager, IV
Schwartz, H., & Rush, B.	*The Diamond Tree*, II
Shannon, G.	*Stories to Solve*, II
	More Stories to Solve, II
Simon, S.	*Space Words*, IV
	Stars, IV
	The Sun, IV
Willson, R. B.	*Merry Christmas!* IV

Appendix B

Cross Reference: Topic

Animals

Aardema, V.	*Traveling to Tondo* (civet cat, pigeon, python, tortoise), II
	Who's in Rabbit's House? II
Allen, L.	*The Mouse Bride*, II
Belpré, P.	*Perez and Martina* (cockroaches), II
Brown, M. W.	*The Runaway Bunny*, I
	Wait Till the Moon is Full (raccoons, rabbits), I
Brusca, M. C.	*On the Pampas* (horses), I
Bryan, A.	*The Cat's Purr*, II
	Turtle Knows Your Name, II
Bunting, E.	*The Sea World Book of Whales*, IV
Caulkins, J. V.	*Pets of the Presidents*, IV
Cleary, B.	*The Mouse and the Motorcycle* and sequels, III
Climo, S.	*King of the Birds*, II
Dahl, R.	*Esio Trot* (tortoise), III
	Minpins (swan), II
Ernst, L. C.	*Ginger Jumps* (dog), I
	Nattie Parsons' Good-Luck Lamb, I
	Walter's Tail (dog), I
Flack, M.	*The Story about Ping* (duck), I
Freeman, L. & D.	*Pet of the Met* (mice), I
Hendry, D.	*A Camel Called April*, I
Hewett, J.	*Laura Loves Horses*, I
Hoban, R.	*The Mouse and His Child*, III
Kherdian, D.	*Feathers and Tails* (birds), II
Kirstein, L.	*Puss in Boots*, II
Leaf, M.	*The Story of Ferdinand* (bull), I
Mansell, D.	*If Dinosaurs Came to Town*, I
Most, B.	*The Littlest Dinosaurs*, I

Polacco, P.	*Mrs. Katz and Tush* (cats), I
Schlein, M.	*The Year of the Panda*, III
Stolz, M.	*King Emmett the Second* (pig), III
Tompert, A.	*Grandfather Tang's Story* (foxes, etc.), I
Van Laan, N.	*A Mouse in My House*, I
	Rainbow Crow, II

The Arts

Ashabranner, B.	*Always to Remember* (architectural design), IV
Donnelly, J.	*A Wall of Names*, IV
Fisher, L. E.	*Alphabet Art*, IV
	Pyramid of the Sun, Pyramid of the Moon, IV
Freeman, L. & D.	*Pet of the Met* (music), I
Godden, R.	*The Valiant Chatti-maker* (pottery), III
Goldstein, P.	*Long Is a Dragon* (Chinese writing), IV
Griffin, P. R.	*Otto from Otherwhere* (music from another planet), III
Knight, M. B.	*Talking Walls*, I
Namioka, L.	*Yang the Youngest and His Terrible Ear*, III
Paterson, K.	*The Master Puppeteer*, III
Rodari, F.	*A Weekend with Picasso* (painting), IV
Say, A.	*The Inn-Keeper's Apprentice* (cartooning), III
Skira-Venturi, R.	*A Weekend with Degas* (painting), IV
Yacowitz, C.	*The Jade Stone* (carving), II

English Language
(See also *Holidays and Special Occasions, Science, Work*, and *Sports and Recreation*.)

Cleary, B.	*Muggie Maggie* (cursive writing), III
MacDonald, S.	*Alphabatics*, I
Maestro, B.	*Delivery Van*, I
	Taxi, I
	Where Is My Friend? I
Most, B.	*There's an Ant in Anthony*, I
Parish, P.	*Amelia Bedelia*, I
	Teach Us, Amelia Bedelia, I
	Thank You, Amelia Bedelia, I
Sarnoff, J.	*Words*, IV
Scarry, R.	*Richard Scarry's Best Word Book Ever*, I

| Terban, M. | *I Think I Thought and Other Tricky Verbs*, IV |
| | *Your Foot's on My Feet*, IV |

Holidays and Special Occasions

Behrens, J.	*Gung Hay Fat Choy* (Chinese New Year), IV
Chaikin, M.	*Ask Another Question* (Passover), IV
	Light Another Candle (Hanukkah), IV
Graham-Barber, L.	*Doodle Dandy* (U.S. Independence Day), IV
	Gobble! (U.S. Thanksgiving Day), IV
	Mushy (Valentine's Day), IV
Greene, C.	*Holidays around the World*, IV
Hendry, D.	*Christmas on Exeter Street*, I
Kelley, E.	*April Fools' Day*, IV
	Christmas around the World, IV
	Happy New Year, IV
Laird, E.	*The Road to Bethlehem* (Christmas), II
Limburg, P. R.	*Weird* (Halloween), IV
Menotti, G. C.	*Amahl and the Night Visitors* (Christmas), III
Perl, L.	*Candles, Cakes, and Donkey Tails* (birthdays), IV
Tompert, A.	*The Silver Whistle* (Christmas), I
Wallace, I.	*Chin Chiang and the Dragon's Dance* (first day of the Year of the Dragon), I
Willson, R. B.	*Merry Christmas!* IV

Science ·

Branley, F. M.	*Neptune* (astronomy), IV
Buck, P. S.	*The Big Wave* (weather), III
Bunting, E.	*The Sea World Book of Whales* (marine ecology), IV
Fisher, L. E.	*Galileo* (astronomy), IV
Freedman, R.	*The Wright Brothers* (aviation), IV
Gibbons, G.	*Weather Words and What They Mean*, I
Greene, C.	*Marco Polo* (exploration), IV
Mansell, D.	*If Dinosaurs Came to Town* (paleontology), I
Meltzer, M.	*Columbus and the World around Him* (exploration), IV
Most, B.	*The Littlest Dinosaurs* (paleontology), I
Pelta, K.	*Discovering Christopher Columbus* (exploration, navigation, historical research), IV
Ride, S.	*To Space and Back*, IV
	Voyager (space science), IV

Schwartz, D. M.	*How Much Is a Million?* (mathematics), IV
	If You Made a Million (mathematics), IV
Simon, S.	*Space Words*, IV
	Stars, IV
	The Sun, IV
Williams, T. T., & Major, T.	*The Secret Language of Snow* (weather), IV

Sports and Recreation

Baker, C. G.	*Fight for Honor* and sequels (karate), III
Brusca, M. C.	*On the Pampas* (horseback riding), I
Freeman, L. & D.	*Pet of the Met* (opera), I
Hewett, J.	*Laura Loves Horses* (horseback riding), I
Leaf, M.	*The Story of Ferdinand* (bullfighting), I
Lord, B. B.	*In the Year of the Boar and Jackie Robinson* (baseball), III
Myers, W. D.	*Me, Mop, and the Moondance Kid* (baseball), III
	Mop, Moondance and the Nagasaki Knights (baseball), III
Namioka, L.	*Yang the Youngest and His Terrible Ear* (baseball), III
Say, A.	*The Bicycle Man* (tricky bicycle riding), I
	El Chino (bullfighting), IV
Scarry, R.	*Richard Scarry's Best Busy Year Ever* (games, gardening, holidays, etc.), I

War

Ashabranner, B.	*Always to Remember* (Vietnam), IV
Baillie, A.	*Little Brother* (Khmer Rouge in Cambodia), III
Berleth, R.	*Samuel's Choice* (American Revolution), III
Choi, S. N.	*Year of Impossible Goodbyes* (World War II), III
Donnelly, J.	*A Wall of Names* (Vietnam), IV
Freedman, R.	*Lincoln* (U.S. Civil War), IV
Fritz, J.	*China's Long March* (China's communist revolution), IV
Garrigue, S.	*The Eternal Spring of Mr. Ito* (World War II), III
Haugaard, E. C.	*The Boy and the Samurai* (feudal Japan), III
	The Samurai's Tale (feudal Japan), III
Heide, F. P., & Gilliland, J. H.	*Sami and the Time of Troubles* (fighting in Lebanon), I
Kent, Z.	*The Story of the Saigon Airlift* (Vietnam), IV

Lowry, L.   *Number the Stars* (World War II), III

Meltzer, M.   *George Washington and the Birth of Our Nation* (American Revolution), IV

Morpurgo, M.   *Waiting for Anya* (World War II), III

Paterson, K.   *Rebels of the Heavenly Kingdom* (Taiping Rebellion, China), III

Watkins, Y. K.   *So Far from the Bamboo Grove* (World War II), III

Whelan, G.   *Goodbye, Vietnam* (refugees), III

Work

Andrews, J.   *The Very Last First Time* (mussel gathering), I

De Paola, T.   *Tony's Bread* (bakery), II

Ernst, L. C.   *Ginger Jumps* (circus), I

Giblin, J. C.   *Chimney Sweeps*, IV

Godden, R.   *The Valiant Chatti-maker* (pottery), III

Heide, F. P., & Gilliland, J. H.   *The Day of Ahmed's Secret* (delivery), I

Krumbold, J.   *. . . and now Miguel* (sheep raising), III

Maestro, B.   *Delivery Van*, I
     Taxi, I

Newton, P.   *The Stonecutter*, II

Say, A.   *The Inn-Keeper's Apprentice* (art), III

Scarry, R.   *Richard Scarry's Busiest People Ever*, I

Yacowitz, C.   *The Jade Stone* (stone carving), II

Yee, P.   *Tales from Gold Mountain* (Chinese railroad workers in the United States), I

Appendix C

Some Useful References

Books

Brown, Dorothy S. (1988). *A world of books: An annotated reading list for ESL/ EFL students*. Alexandria, VA: TESOL.

Christison, Mary Ann. (1982). *English through poetry*. Hayward, CA: Alemany.

Coody, Betty, & Nelson, David. (1982). *Teaching elementary language arts: A literature approach*. Prospect Heights, IL: Waveland.

Devine, Joanne, Carrell, Patricia, & Eskey, David. (Eds.). (1987). *Research in reading in English as a second language*. Alexandria, VA: TESOL.

Donavin, Denise Perry (ed.). (1992). *Best of the best for children*. American Library Association. New York, Toronto, London, Sydney, Auckland: Random House.

Hearne, Betsy. (1981, rev. ed. 1990). *Choosing books for children: A commonsense guide*. New York: Delacorte.

Hepler, Susan. (1993). *Children's literature in the elementary school* (5th ed.). New York: Harcourt.

Landsberg, Michele. (1987, rev. ed. 1989). *Reading for the fun of it: Best books for young readers*. New York: Prentice-Hall. (paper)

Lipson, Eden Ross (ed.). (1991). *New York Times parent's guide to the best books for children*. New York: Random House.

Lurie, Alison. (1990). *Don't tell the grown-ups: Subversive children's literature*. Boston, Toronto, London: Little, Brown. Paper, with subtitle *Why kids love the books they do*. New York: Avon, 1990.

Nilsen, Eden Ross (ed.). (1991). *Your reading: A booklist for junior high and middle school students* (8th ed.). Urbana, IL: National Council of Teachers of English.

Rigg, Pat, & Enright, Scott D. (eds.). (1988). *Children and ESL: Integrating perspectives*. Alexandria, VA: TESOL.

Smallwood, Betty Ansin. (1991). *The literature connection: A read-aloud guide for multicultural classrooms*. New York: Addison-Wesley.

Townsend, John Rowe. (1992). *Written for children: An outline of English language children's literature* (3rd rev. ed.). New York: Harper & Row. (paper)

Trelease, Jim. (1989). *The new read-aloud handbook* (2nd rev. ed.). New York: Viking. (paper)

Periodicals

Book Links. Chicago: American Library Association. (bimonthly)

The Horn Book Guide. Boston. (published in February and September)

The Horn Book Magazine. Boston. (bimonthly)

Also available from TESOL

All Things to All People:
A Primer for K-12 ESL Teachers in Small Programs
Donald C. Flemming, Lucie C. Germer, and Christiane Kelley

A New Decade of Language Testing Research:
Selected Papers From
the 1990 Language Testing Research Colloquium
Dan Douglas and Carol Chapelle, Editors

Common Threads of Practice:
Teaching English to Children Around the World
Katharine Davies Samway and Denise McKeon, Editors

Dialogue Journal Writing with Nonnative English Speakers:
A Handbook for Teachers
Joy Kreeft Peyton and Leslee Reed

Dialogue Journal Writing with Nonnative English Speakers:
An Instructional Packet for Teachers and Workshop Leaders
Joy Kreeft Peyton and Jana Staton

Directory of Professional Preparation Programs
in TESOL in the United States, 1992–1994
Helen Kornblum, with Ellen Garshick, Editors

Discourse and Performance of International Teaching Assistants
Carolyn G. Madden and Cynthia L. Myers, Editors

Diversity as Resource:
Redefining Cultural Literacy
Denise E. Murray, Editor

New Ways in Teacher Education
Donald Freeman, with Steve Cornwell, Editors

New Ways in Teaching Reading
Richard R. Day, Editor

New Ways in Teaching Vocabulary
Paul Nation, Editor

Students and Teachers Writing Together:
Perspectives on Journal Writing
Joy Kreeft Peyton, Editor

Video in Second Language Teaching:
Using, Selecting, and Producing Video for the Classroom
Susan Stempleski and Paul Arcario, Editors

A World of Books: An Annotated Reading List for ESL/EFL Students
Dorothy S. Brown

For more information, contact
Teachers of English to Speakers of Other Languages, Inc.
1600 Cameron Street, Suite 300
Alexandria, Virginia 22314 USA
Tel 703-836-0774 Fax 703-836-7864